Algorithmic Trading

Tricks to Learn and Win With Algorithmic Trading

(The Completely New Guide to Machine Learning for Algorithmic Trading)

Tracey Davis

Published By **Oliver Leish**

Tracey Davis

Algorithmic Trading: Tricks to Learn and Win With Algorithmic Trading (The Completely New Guide to Machine Learning for Algorithmic Trading)

ISBN 978-1-77485-733-5

No part of this guidebook shall be reproduced in any form without permission in writing from the publisher except in the case of brief quotations embodied in critical articles or reviews.

Legal & Disclaimer

The information contained in this ebook is not designed to replace or take the place of any form of medicine or professional medical advice. The information in this ebook has been provided for educational & entertainment purposes only.

The information contained in this book has been compiled from sources deemed reliable, and it is accurate to the best of the Author's knowledge; however, the Author cannot guarantee its accuracy and validity and cannot be held liable for any errors or omissions. Changes are periodically made to this book. You must consult your doctor or get professional medical advice before using any of the suggested remedies, techniques, or information in this book.

Upon using the information contained in this book, you agree to hold harmless the Author from and against any damages, costs, and expenses, including any legal fees potentially resulting from the application of any of the information provided by this guide. This disclaimer applies to any damages or injury caused by the use and application, whether directly or indirectly, of any advice or information presented, whether for breach of contract, tort, negligence, personal injury, criminal intent, or under any other cause of action.

You agree to accept all risks of using the information presented inside this book. You need to consult a professional medical practitioner in order to ensure you are both able and healthy enough to participate in this program.

TABLE OF CONTENTS

Introduction

The distinction between the two will give you a complete picture of the experience of trading. Let's say you flip the coin 50 times. It has turned head 49 times. If you now seek out a statistician to determine what is the likelihood of flipping heads once more. The statistician will give you 1/2. If you meet a trader to request the same and the trader will inform you that there's an 80% chance you'll flip heads once more. If you inquire about why they believe this is real, he will inform you that there's no way that a coin can always be a head 49 times every time the coin is turned. It is biased, and that means there is the possibility for it to show heads every time you flip it. This is the way traders think and that is the way you should think as well.

It is essential to ensure that you're ahead of the rest on the market The best method for this is by creating software for trading algorithms. This book provides a comprehensive guide to the algorithmic trading software and strategies you can apply. Algorithmic trading took the financial market by storm. If you're looking to know more about algorithmic trading, then you are in the right location. This book will provide you with the information you need and assist you in understanding the concept of algorithmic trading.

Through this book, you'll discover the basic principles in algorithmic trading. Additionally, you will learn about the various strategies can be used if you would like to develop algorithms for trading models. Many people are unaware of the places they can make use of algorithmic trading on the market. This book sheds insight into the various strategies that are used for algorithmic trading. If you're looking to be an expert in algorithmic trading you'll need to learn certain abilities, and these abilities are described within the text. One of the most crucial capabilities you should improve is your programming skills. Since the majority of algorithms employ Python the book provides some insight into the basics of Python. The examples in this book use Python.

You will discover that algorithmic trading operates similar to artificial intelligence in that the program you design will be self-aware and adjust. When this occurs it is that no intervention from a human necessary. You are able to follow invisibly buying and selling orders software puts in. You may choose to utilize an algorithmic trading program that has already been created or build one yourself. There are a variety of tools available for the latter.

The truth is that any algorithmic trading strategy can't be relied on without a doubt until you have backtested the strategy. Only after you have done this that you can ensure that the model is operating correctly. This book also sheds information on how to verify the model you create or apply to.

Chapter 1: An Introduction To Algorithmic Trading

Algorithmic trading, like its name suggests, is an order or procedures that traders is required to follow to execute the trade. The trade is able to generate profits with a speed and frequency that humans cannot compete with. This is the reason that many traders prefer to make use of this type of trading. The steps or instructions you follow is based on amount, time, price and other mathematical models. In addition to these benefits for traders algorithms make trading more systematic , and makes market more liquid. It also helps rule out any influence human emotions could influence trading decisions.

A. The Practice of Algorithmic Trading

Let's suppose that the trader follows these steps to trade:

A person buys 100 shares of an investment when the moving average of 50 days is higher than that of the moving average for 250 days. If you're unfamiliar about moving averages we'll describe what they're utilized to do. Moving averages are the sum of all data points in the past. It utilizes these data points to identify the variations between the information points. This will allow it to be easy to determine the trend.

He or she decides to dispose of these shares if the average of moving averages after 50 days drops below those of 200 days.

If you feed the system using these basic instructions, it will keep track of how much the shares are trading using the indicators of moving average. It will then place buy and sell order on these stocks in accordance with the requirements it fulfills. The trader does not have to keep track of these rates or charts. The trader does not need to work on placing order to buy or sell by hand. The system will identify the most profitable trading opportunity based upon the requirements that the trader has set within the system.

The advantages of algorithmic trading

The following are some of the advantages of trading using algorithms:

The trade will always be made based on the most optimal price

The orders that are placed on trades are precise and quick. There is a chance of earning the amount you desire from the orders.

Because the trade is executed in a timely manner it is not affected by major price changes.

The transaction cost will decrease

* The software will be able to check the market conditions

The chance of making manual mistakes will be reduced since the algorithm works using information

The algorithm can be tested reverse-wards using both real-time and historical data. This gives the trader the chance to determine if the strategy employed is feasible

The method can help reduce the mistakes made by traders due to emotional and psychological aspects.

We will discuss the advantages more in depth later in our book. The majority of trading algorithms are high-frequency trading algorithm. They attempt to take advantage of the variance between marketplaces by placing transactions at fast speed on various markets. These orders are according to preprogrammed guidelines.

Where can Algorithmic Trading Be Used?

It is possible to use this kind of trading in any type of investment and trading which includes:

Systematic Trading

A few examples of systematic traders include hedge fund investors, pair traders and trend followers. A pair trader employs strategies that match the short and long position in a pair instruments that are highly connected with each other, such as currencies, stocks and exchange traded funds. They will be able to easily programme the rules they would like to implement when they put orders to buy or sell on stocks. They can then employ these rules to create the trades in a way that is automatic.

Long-Term - Mid-Term Investors

The types of investors mentioned above are also known as buy-side investors and include mutual fund investors and insurance company investors as well as pension fund investors. They employ this form of trading to buy stocks in large amounts. They use this technique when they wish to affect the prices of stock with massive quantities and different instruments.

Short-Term Traders

A short-term trader also known as a sell-side participant is an arbitrageur, or market makers, similar to a brokerage house or an investor. They benefit from the ability to execute their trades on a regular basis. Furthermore the type of trading can help create an adequate level of liquidity for sellers on the market.

Algorithmic trading provides trader with a system to make trades on the market. This method allows you to trade on data from the past and not based on intuition or influence.

Algorithmic Trading Strategies

Every strategy you create or employ for trading algorithms will require you to find the opportunities that can be profitable by reducing cost and increasing profits. This chapter will cover some of the most popular algorithmic trading strategies that are used. We will discuss a few of them in greater detail in the future book.

Strategies to Follow Trends

This is among the most commonly used methods that all algorithms based trading programs rely on. These include Moving averages, price level fluctuations channel breakouts, channel indicators, and various other indicators of technical nature. These are the most basic ways to implement algorithms in trading since they don't need the program to anticipate any price movement. The trade is initiated once the desired trend is observed. It is possible to include trends in algorithms for trading without needing to add sophisticated predictive analysis. The most popular methods is to employ the 50-day or 200-day moving average.

Arbitrage Opportunities

Some traders prefer to invest in multiple markets. They might buy a stock at a lower price in one market, and then sell the same stock on another market for a more expensive price. The difference in price or the profit they earn is not risky and is referred to as arbitrage. You can repeat the process for future investments as well as stocks, since price differentials are likely to be present. If you use an algorithm to detect this price difference and then you can place these orders with efficiency, you could profit.

Balance of the Index Fund

Each index fund has set time frames that it can be adjusted. This allows traders to bring their portfolios up to the level of the indexes which they've set as their benchmark. This can create a lucrative chance for an algorithmic trader. The trader could place an order and provide from twenty to eight basis points, based on the quantity of stocks that are within the fund prior to when it is adjusted. The system initiates the transactions, meaning that the trader could make massive profits at the highest cost.

Strategies based on mathematical Models

The delta-neutral strategy for trading is a well-tested mathematical strategy, as well as other strategies, allows traders to employ various combinations to any security. This is also a strategy for portfolios which consists of several positions. It permits traders to reduce positive and negative deltas by using a ratio that will measure the fluctuation in the price of an asset against an increase in the value for its derivative. The total delta should be zero, however this isn't the norm.

Trade Range or Mean Reversion

There is a belief that price fluctuations of stocks are just temporary. The value of a stock is often returned to its average or mean value over the course of a time. Mean reversion strategies are an underlying theory. A trader who is algorithmic can create an application that allows to determine and define the price range, and then indicate that system it is required to make an order for an inventory or asset.

VWAP, also known as Volume-Weighted Average Price

The VWAP strategy will permit the trader to break down an order into smaller parts and then release the segments to the market using certain previous volume patterns that are unique to the stock. The goal of this algorithm for trading is to create the order most closely aligned with the VWAP.

TWAP or Time-Wooded Average Price

It is the TWAP is a technique that is like the VWAP strategy in that the algorithm will split a large order into smaller parts. With this strategy, however the algorithm releases the segments based on a set of specified time frames. The goal for the algorithm is complete the order at a time when the cost of the shares is near to its average value. This can reduce the impact of the market on the stock.

POV, also known as Percentage of Volume

If you employ this method the algorithm will issue partial orders towards a particular stock until the order for trade is completed. This partial order is made in accordance with the specified participation ratio dependent on the amount of stocks traded on the market. The other strategy is to make an order based on an amount that is based on the amount of stock traded that is traded and then decrease or increase it as it is determined that the value of the share has reached the desired level.

Implementation Shortfall

When you make an order on a particular stock on the market, you'll be charged a fee because there's always a delay when placing the exact same order on the market in real-time. If you employ this method this algorithm will instantly make the order available in the market in real-time. This will reduce the cost of your order and also allow you to profit from the potential price that comes with delayed execution. If prices of stock changes in a positive direction the algorithm will increase the participation rate while decreasing the rate in other cases.

Other Strategies

Certain algorithms are employed in order to discover the dynamics behind the scenes. These algorithms are known as sniffing algorithms. They are also known as they are equipped with the appropriate software and code that allows it to determine the existence of identical algorithms that are on the opposite side. If you employ these algorithms to calculate the price of the stocks on the marketplace, you could profit from filling orders at higher prices. This is also referred to as front-running.

Technical Requirements

It is necessary to create an application on your computer to create an algorithm. This is the most important part in this kind of trading. The next step is to test your algorithm using historical data to determine whether the strategy actually is effective. The goal or challenge is to change the method that was developed into a computerized method that allows users to login to any trading account to place an order. The requirements for algorithmic trading include:

• Computer programming skills to design an effective trading strategy. You may also engage developers to create the code for you , or make use of an existing program

• Access to certain trading platforms, where you can place an order

Connectivity to the network

Access to market information that allows you to observe how the algorithm is changing so that you can determine the ideal time to place an order.

Infrastructure and the capability to test your algorithm in the backend after you have built it. It is essential to backtest it prior to letting your algorithm go live on the market

• Collect historical data which you can use as a backtest for the algorithm. The quantity of historical data you collect will differ according to the complexity of the algorithm.

Exemples of Algorithmic Trading

Let's take a look at an example. RDS also known as Royal Dutch Shell is a company which is listed on the LSE as well as the London Stock Exchange and AEX or Amsterdam Stock Exchange. Every trader would like to take advantage of arbitrage opportunities in order to make investments on this particular stock. Now let's begin creating an algorithm that can let traders recognize this possibility. These are the key points that we must take into consideration:

LSE trades in British pounds sterling, whereas AEX is only trading in euros

Because of the different time zone between these two nations which means that the LSE will be opened at the same time as AEX and the shares trade on both markets at the same time for a couple of hours. Trading will continue for one hour on the LSE following the time that AEX closes.

Are you thinking you could make use of arbitrage trading using the RDS stock, which is traded on these exchanges in various currencies? Here are a few conditions you must take into consideration:

• A program or script which allows you to see the latest prices on the market.

The price feeds from the two AEX and LSE

Foreign exchange feed or feed on forex rates for EUR-GBP.

The process or route that must be followed to make the buy or sell orders on the stock

Verifying the algorithm with an ability to backtest

Your algorithm, or the program you design must perform the following functions:

Check out the coming prices of shares both on those of the LSE and AEX exchanges.

Make use of an exchange rate in order to convert cost of the stock from one currency to another.

If there's an amount of difference which is sufficient to offer a lucrative opportunity then the algorithm or program must put the buy or sell order for the stock on the exchange that is cheaper or more expensive exchange, respectively.

A profit from arbitrage will occur when the algorithm or program will correctly execute the order

This is a simple thing isn't it? The actual practice of algorithmic trading is however, quite different. It's difficult to implement or even maintain. Keep in mind that if one trader has access to an algorithmic trading system and others can, too. It is crucial to keep in mind that prices change in milliseconds, or microseconds. In the above example suppose that you've completed an order to buy however, what do you suppose will happen if are unable to execute the sell trade by using the algorithm to determine when is the appropriate moment to place the order? As an individual trader, you'll only have the option of changing your strategy to render the arbitrage trading useless.

There are other issues and risks such as problems with network connectivity and system failure risk as well as flawed algorithms. the time-lag between placing an order and fulfilling that trade. If you are developing a complex algorithm, you must do a rigorous backtesting procedure to make sure that the algorithm is well-developed.

Intelligent Algorithmic Trading Models

In this article we will take a look at one of the top sophisticated algorithmic trading strategies.

When you think about algorithms or trading systems, you can comprehend the concepts easily using an easy structure made up of four parts. Each component will take care of a specific element of an algorithmic trading model, including the strategy handler trade execution handler, as well as the data handler. They can be connected to one another in a variety of ways, and we'll discuss each one of these components more thoroughly as we go along.

Data Component

This algorithmic trading platform, as all other computer systems, can use any type of data. This means you can utilize semi-structured, structured unstructured, and any of the three kinds of data. In the event that data are structured it is a sign that there's some sort of organization in the data. Examples include JSON documents, CSV files, spreadsheets database, XML file and various other types of data structure. Market-related information such as trade volumes, prices for interdays price, intra-day prices, and the prices at the end of each day are accessible with structured format. Economic and financial data of companies are also accessible as structured files. You can get financial data which is structured through Morningstar as well as Quandl. If the data isn't well-organized, it's not structured data. Examples include news, social media audio and video. This kind of data can be difficult to handle, and usually requires process of data mining as well as data analytics techniques to analyze the data. Because people frequently use information and news on websites such as Facebook and Twitter to trade and trading, there are tools being developed to comprehend this kind of data more effectively. A majority of these tools utilize artificial intelligence techniques such as neural networks to understand the meaning of the information.

Model Component

The model you create represents the world and all the data present in that world in the eyes of the algorithmic trading systems. Financial models will reflect the assumptions of the algorithmic system on the way that markets function. The aim in any system is to make use of this data to draw some conclusions regarding the global economy. In this instance we're just interested in understanding the ways that markets function. It is crucial to realize that the majority of models you create are not correct and only a small portion models will be beneficial to you.

It is possible to construct a model by using a variety of techniques and methods. They are all similar in that they all accomplish one thing: they simplify the system to an understandable and quantifiable rule set that define how the system performs under different scenarios. These approaches can include fuzzy and symbolic logic systems such as neural networks, mathematical models and induction rule sets and even decision trees.

Mathematical Models

If you employ mathematical models to comprehend the way markets behave you are creating the most accurate financial model. The majority model are built on the notion that prices in the market will change over time, by relying on a stochastic process. This implies that each market is unpredictable. This is a valid assumption to base your business on and is a great hypothesis to build. Each derivative pricing model as well as certain valuation models are based upon this assumption.

The majority of quantitative models suggest that only a random risk factor determines the returns for any securities. The extent to which these returns are affected can be described as sensitivity. For example, if you have a diverse portfolio and you are able to get a good return, the returns you get could be influenced by interest rates that are short-term as well as the general performance of the stock market, returns from your entire portfolio, or a variety of forex rates. These factors can be understood by studying historical data and then create an algorithm that simulates the risks. The model will also determine the risks that risk factors do and help predict the return of the portfolio.

Fuzzy and Symbolic models of logic

Symbolic logic is a form of reasoning that requires you to analyze predicates as logic statements made with operators such as XOR, AND, and OR and then evaluate the results. It will be be false or true. Fuzzy logic does not just examine only the binary output - either true or false. It will also determine a grade for all of the above predicates. These degrees can be defined according to a set membership functions.

In the case of market conditions, your information that you provide to the system may include indicators that are believed to be in a relationship with one another. These indicators determine the value of the security. They could be fundamental, technical quantitative, or any other form. For example fuzzy logic systems make use of historical data to conclude that the exponentially moving average of five days is higher than the average of 10 days. When this occurs, then the returns of the stock will rise by 65% over the coming five days. The rules can be identified with a rule-induction set. The set is similar to the decision tree, however the outcomes will be in the form of a human-readable format.

Decision Tree Models

Decision tree models are similar to the induction rules set. It is only different that rules are designed by an equilateral tree, with the output being binary. The binary tree has in which there only two outputs. That means that each node of the tree will just have 2 outputs. The outputs are known as left and right children. The node represents the boundary of decision or rule, while the child node represents the output. Classification and regression trees comprise two kinds of trees for making decisions. A classification tree has distinct classes and a regression tree can have different outcomes for a particular variable. The type of information used to build a decision tree will decide the kind of output you will get. This will, in turn, determine the type of decision tree that is created. The algorithms that are used to construct the decision tree include C4.5 and genetic programming. C4.5. Like rule induction, all inputs used in the decision tree model will contain all the relevant data related to a specific technological or statistical aspect. These variables determine the returns on any stock.

Neural Network Models

Neural networks are among the most well-known machine learning models utilized by traders using algorithms. Each neural network is built exactly the same way as neurons inside the brain. There are several layers of neurons connected via nodes. Each of these layers represent an output and input layer. Each node is known as a perceptron. they are linear. But when you add an activation function as well as weights for these neurons, they'll no longer be linear. If you employ an unrecurrent neural network the perceptrons are split into layers. Each of these layers is connected to the other.

Each neural network is comprised of three layers: the hidden, input and the output layer. There can be multiple hidden layers in the neural network. Like the name implies, the input layer receives the input variables. And for an algorithmic trading system, the input variables must be ones that influence the security. Output layers will contain the buy sell, hold or buy orders or any possible results. The hidden layer will include the weights that are associated with the input variables, which will help minimize the error that is uncovered during backtesting. Hidden layers are employed to identify salient characteristics from the data and then they are used to determine the results.

Other decision models can be utilized to construct algorithms for trading models. These models can be used to forecast the results for any input variable based upon the probabilities of the value of the stock. The kind of model you select can affect the automated trading strategy. It is possible to utilize multiple models to improve precision, however this can add complexity to the implementation.

It is important to remember that your model acts as the heart for the algorithms and if you wish to make the system smart it must be able to keep all the data about its performance, including mistakes. The model needs to be able to learn how to adjust based on the information it accumulates.

Execution Component

If the algorithmic trading program decides on the stocks it will place an order on, the execution component will put the trade's order. The component has to meet the non-functional and functional specifications that are part of an algorithmic trading platform. For example the frequency with when it makes the trade on the trade as well as the speed of execution as well as the process by the order is sent through the exchange as well as the duration during which the trade is being held must be taken into consideration. Each algorithmic trading program must be able to meet these criteria.

Monitor Component

A function that is objective is one that allows the system to measure its own performance by using quantitative indicators. Artificial intelligence is trained through these tasks. In the field of finance, the metrics of returns adjusted for risk include three ratios: Sharpe ratio Treynor ratio and Sortino ratio. The model component will focus to maximize one of these ratios. The problem with this is the fact that markets are constantly changing or random, so models, logic, and neural networks that have worked before are likely to fail. To counter this the algorithmic trading model must always be trained by using the information provided by models themselves. It is this kind of self-awareness which will allow the model to be able to adapt to changes in its surroundings.

Chapter 2: The Benefits Of Algorithmic Trading

Once you have mastered the fundamentals of algorithmic trading, we will take a look at the benefits and drawbacks of making use of this method for trading.

Benefits

Reduce the impact of emotions

A trading algorithmic system or automated trading software can help to limit the influence of emotions on trading. The traders who don't use algorithmic trading software frequently allow their emotions to guide to them into trading. The trade is made automatically by the software if the criteria for making trades are satisfied. Automated trading, apart from helping traders make the best trades, also allows traders to regulate how much money invests in the market for stocks. The software for trading will only place an order when it sees an chance.

Ability to test back-tests

Backtesting applies trade rules on the software based on historic market information. These tests serve to determine the validity of the software for trading. When you create an algorithmic trading program you must ensure you have rules that are completely clear. There should be no confusion or any room for interpretation. It is impossible for a computer to figure out what it has to accomplish. A trader will then be able to check these rules based on past data before deciding to put his money into the market. If a trader backtests using an algorithmic program the trader can identify the likelihood of success for the software. This is the sum the trader is able to be able to win or lose with each amount of risk.

Maintain discipline

The rules that software has to adhere to are clearly defined commas and the execution of trades is done in a way that is automated. This means that the discipline of trading will remain in place even when the market conditions are volatile. If traders don't use algorithms, they are often lose money due to emotions like fear of losing money or the desire to make more money from trading. Automated trading ensures that traders are disciplined as every decision is by relying on a specific set of guidelines. Additionally the errors that occur when using chart readers are reduced. The software also makes sure that each and every data entry is correctly entered in the system.

Keep Consistent

Many traders struggle to plan their trades and trade on the basis of their plans. If a trader does not follow the rules that alter the expectation of the strategy, a plan that is guaranteed to succeed will be a failure. It is not possible for that a trading strategy will win every time you employ it. Keep in mind that losses are an aspect of trading. But it is important to recognize that losses can cause trauma psychologically. Let's suppose that an investor has had to suffer loss twice in consecutive days. This trader might decide to not make his next visit. If the next trade would have brought the trader an advantage, the probability of the system will be reduced by 45% because the trader decided to not make this trade. Because algorithmic trading is automated it is imperative that the trader adhere to his strategy.

Increased Speed of Placing Orders

Be aware that computers react immediately to any situation that change. This means that algorithms in trading software will generate the correct orders when that any of the requirements meet. Be aware that every minute can be a source of noise when it concerns trading. Just a few seconds can be a significant difference. Once a position is input into the software, orders are generated automatically. These orders contain profits targets and stop losses. The market is likely to move quickly. If the market requires the protection of your stop loss levelbefore you are able to make the purchase it could demoralize you. A trading algorithm software can ensure that this doesn't happen.

Diversification

A trader is able to employ multiple strategies and even trade in different markets, if they choose to utilize algorithms in their trading software. This will enable traders to spread risk among different instruments, creating a hedge against losing positions. It's hard for humans to manage this kind of trade successfully, unlike computers. Computers are able to scan the market and search for the best trading opportunity across various markets. This helps computers track trades and easily create the appropriate orders to generate profits.

Time and Talent

The option of discretion to generate huge profits if they had the time, money and the right sources. If you're using an automated system, you will not need an analyst to follow market's news and the changes in prices. As traders, you have the ability to use a variety of strategies to use the information it collects from the market to help you make the right choices if you are using an algorithmic trading program. The software can help you to develop new markets and strategies which will help you expand your investment portfolio. Additionally, you can do position sizing and dynamic management of disks in real time. These are extremely complicated tasks. A trading system that is automated can respond to any market event faster than humans. Computers don't require bio break or a sleep. If you do not turn off the power on, your computer will function normally.

Negatives

Costs will rise

If you are planning to utilize brokers to conduct trading in the future, you'll need to pay more in order to implement an algorithmic approach to trading. The situation is slowly changing because other traders are using algorithmic trading strategies. The majority of traders are now using an XIX protocol. The protocol outlines guidelines on which traders can conduct transactions through a myriad of exchanges. Another cost that traders will have to pay will be the expense of maintaining data.

Every trader must examine large amounts of data in order to come up with the most effective strategy. If you wish lower costs of trading by focusing on equity. If you're an experienced trader, you should buy an actual data feed. It is going to cost you more. The main difference between these two products is their latency. A trading company will be competing with another company to determine who is able to move or make an order first on the market. If you do not have trade software to manage your trading activities, you could have to go to the exchange in order to place your order. Additionally, the time between your workplace and the place of business can increase the time. This is not the case if you intend to only engage with high-frequency trades. It is, however, necessary to require a computer connected to a reliable Internet connection that is able to run multiple displays , and has the most recent Operating System, Backup systems , and an extremely high RAM.

Mechanical failures

The algorithmic trading process does seem very easy. All you have to do is to set up the software, set the rules, get an efficient computer system, have a reliable Internet connection and let the program work its magic.

But this method of trading is a sure thing. Based on the system the trader invests in the software can be residing on a computer, and not on the server. A loss in connectivity would mean that the trader's order will not be put on the market. The algorithmic trading technique can also generate theoretic trades. There could be a distinction between these hypothetical trades and the actual transactions. When using an automated trading system, you need to allow the program to learn. This is why you must start trading with small amounts until you have mastered this technique.

Monitoring

It's best to turn off your computer and go home , since the software that algorithmically trades will be monitoring the trades. However it is still necessary to keep an eye on the software as there's a chance of mechanical problems like power loss and computer crashes or connectivity issues. It is also essential to keep track of any system glitches. Keep in mind that algorithmsic trading software may also encounter glitches. This can result in the absence of orders, duplicate orders, or incorrect orders. If you keep an eye on systems, you are able to eliminate these mistakes and correct them once you spot them.

Over-Optimization

Any trader who utilizes backtesting methods can create the best trading strategy. They can develop a trading program that appears amazing on paper, but it doesn't have to perform well on the market. Over-optimization is the over application of data to an underlying curve. This can result in a faulty trading strategy. You can, for instance, modify a strategy based upon the past to achieve the best results. There is a belief among traders that any algorithmic trading program must always yield a profit. There shouldn't be any issue with the software. To achieve it, the trader could alter the parameters in order to come up with an approach which is nearly perfect. The plan, however, will be ineffective the moment it is put into the market. An investor who is using an automated trading strategy accessible on a server may use the algorithmic software directly through a server-based trading platform. These platforms can provide commercial strategies traders could use. They also will allow the trader to design most suitable strategies.

Chapter 3: Tips To Choose The Best Algorithmic Trading Software

Once you are aware of the various strategies utilized in the development of an algorithmic trading system, Let's take a look at who utilizes an algorithmic trading system and how to select the best one for your needs.

Who uses it?

Large trading companies like hedge funds and investment banks employ algorithmic trading. They are able to do this because they have an abundance of resources within their company. They are able to either develop their own software, or purchase software. They always have massive trading systems, supported by personnel and data centers that are dedicated to their customers.

Individual traders , like quants and skilled proprietary traders typically employ algorithms for trading. The typical proprietary trader is less technologically adept. That means he may opt to buy a pre-made software that can meet any need for trading. You can either buy this software from third-party vendors or select the one provided by their broker. As quants have a good understanding of computer programming as well as trading, they can create the software themselves.

Do I need to build or purchase Software?

You can purchase an algorithmic trading system or develop it yourself. If you decide to purchase an accessible software that you can do is tailor it according to your requirements. The software for trading is usually costly and may have a number of loopholes. If you fail to take care of these loopholes, you're guaranteed to suffer losses. The expense of software can often be a drain on the profits you earn from trading. When you create your algorithmic trading system and you'll need to invest a significant amount hours trying to learn about this tool. It is also necessary to have an in-depth understanding of trading, but that knowledge isn't always enough.

Key Features

Algorithmic trading is an automated method of trading which means that the risk is very high. This is the reason that it is possible to suffer huge losses. It is important to be familiar with the many characteristics of the trading model whatever you opt to build it or purchase it.

Data Accessibility

Rememberthat any trading algorithm you create will always be based on current market prices and information. Some software programs include details on the company's fundamentals, such as the ratio of earnings to price and the earnings per share. Any program you employ to conduct algorithmic trading will analyze the real-time market as well as company data. This data must be integrated into the system when developing the software. The data must be integrated into the system or be designed in such a way that it is able to take data from different sources.

Connectivity to different Markets

A trader looking to trade on multiple markets must understand that the data feeds provided by the markets will differ. This means that their data feeds are also available in a different format , like Multicast, FIX, or TCP/IP. The algorithmic software you choose to use must be able to accept different formats for data. It is also possible to do this with third-party data suppliers such as Reuters and Bloomberg. These companies offer software that permits you to collect market data from multiple exchanges. They also permit you to offer an aggregated output to customers. The algorithmic trading program will be able to process the data as required.

Latency

The latency factor is among the main aspects to take into account when deciding to utilize algorithmic trading. The term "latency" refers to the time interval between the movement of the data point.

Functions to Write Programs

The most popular programming languages that are used to create algorithms to trade are Python, Matlab, Java, Perl, and C++. Third-party sellers sell trading software. They also permit you to make use of customized programs to create your own strategies. Traders can also play on these platforms , and then trade the various concepts they create.

Backtesting of Historical Data

If you are conducting backtesting, it is necessary to test the trading strategy is formulated with previous data. This will enable you to test the efficiency and effectiveness of the strategy using previous data. This will enable you to certify the strategy and determine the need for any modifications. Every trader has to use this method and collect the necessary data required to execute this strategy.

Integration with Trading Interface

The software for algorithmic trading will automatically place trades on the market based upon certain requirements. The program will require the required connectivity that allows traders to place the desired trade directly to the marketplace. To accomplish this, the software must have a connection to the exchange's networks.

Integrating Plug-n'Play

Traders can make use of Matlab software for any type of trend analysis and the Bloomberg terminal to conduct any price analysis as well as the broker's terminal to make the appropriate trades. Based on your individual requirements the software you design should incorporate the integration that is required. Additionally, it should include APIs for various trading platforms. This will allow for the integration as well as the ability to scale.

Platform-Independent Programming

It is necessary to master programming languages in order to create an algorithm. Certain of these programming languages also require a special platform. For instance, certain varieties that use C++ will only be compatible with specific operating systems whereas Perl can be used on Perl across all operating systems. When you purchase or construct trading software, it is best to be looking at software that is not tied to the platform. Alternately, you could select one that is compatible with the majority of languages. There is no way to know of how your trading strategies and strategies change.

Stuff to put under the Hood

There's a saying that monkeys can also press one button to place any purchase or sell order. You must ensure that your dependence on your computer isn't blind. As an investor, you have be aware of what exactly is going on when the computer is making the trade. If you decide to purchase the trading software it is recommended that you read the entire documentation of the software used for trading. This will allow you to understand the basic logic behind every algorithms-based trading strategies. Avoid using strategies that are confusing and are a black box. Don't use them even if the creator declares it to be an effective method to make money.

When creating software, it is important to be honest about the software you intend to implement. It is also important to know the scenarios you're willing to confront using this program. Be sure to backtest the algorithm prior to putting your money in the market.

How Do You Begin?

Any algorithmic trading program that is available offers a no-cost functionality or the option of a trial for a short time. It is also possible to get all the features during a trial. You must download these software and play around with them before you buy them. Be sure to read the manual thoroughly.

If you're looking to design your own trading strategy then you should look into the trading method used by Quantopian. The service provides an online platform through which you can design and test different algorithms in the process of algorithmic trading. It is also possible to create and test a totally new algorithm. This service will be discussed in the next section in depth. The platform will make it easy to test any algorithm you design on market-based data.

The Bottom Line

Algorithmic trading software is expensive, and difficult to develop as you must master various tools and techniques to use while making the algorithm. If you buy ready-made software, you'll be able to save time. But, if you create your own algorithm you can modify the algorithms to meet your requirements. Before you begin looking into algorithms for trading using real money, you must ensure you understand the basic functions of the program you're using. If you don't accomplish this, you could be liable for huge losses.

classification of Algorithmic Trading

It is possible to categorize the various algorithmic trading strategies in the following categories:

"Arbitrage Algorithmic trading" Strategies

Trend-following Algorithmic Trading Strategies or Momentum-based Strategies

Market Algorithmic Trading Strategies

Strategies for Trading Statistically Arbitrage

Let's take a examine the different strategies that are available and the various modeling concepts for each one of these strategies.

Arbitrage Strategies

Let's suppose that a second company is buying an pharmaceutical company. This purchase could raise the value of the stocks of the pharmaceutical corporation since this is a corporate occasion. If you're looking to invest based on pricing inefficiencies that you invest in, then you're using the strategy of events. Spin-offs or mergers, acquisitions and bankruptcy as a trigger upon which to base the investment plan. These strategies for trading will be completely market-neutral, as well as proprietary as hedge fund investors employ these strategies extensively.

Statistics Arbitrage

There are instances that you might be able to profit from an arbitrage opportunity because of a miscalculation in the pricing quoted in the market. If you are using an algorithmic trading method, you can utilize this strategy for your benefit. The chances are only there for short periods of time since market prices can be changed very quickly. This is why it is imperative it is recommended to employ an algorithmic strategy for trading. Machines can monitor the changes in a short time and make the most of these changes. For example, if price of shares offered by Apple drops below $1 the share price of Microsoft will drop by $0.75

However, this doesn't mean Microsoft's share price Microsoft will decrease. Therefore, you are able to trade the Microsoft shares that you have to earn an income.

The Paradigms of Statistics Arbitrage

As we mentioned You can make money from mispricing markets for stocks. One of the best ways to explain statistical arrangment is that you take the risk of a trade across assets that are short-term for a limited time. An investor will benefit from this due to the law of massive numbers. The majority of statistical algorithms are built on pairs of stocks and employ the hypothesis of mean reversion.

Ideas for Modeling

The most common strategies for strategic arbitrage use pairs trading. In this strategy, you'll always be looking at two stocks whose price has changed over time. These two stocks are linked by analyzing the market and their fundamental similarities. This strategy is based on the assumption that the price relative to stocks on the market will be in equilibrium. It is the market's job to adjust any deviation from this equilibrium. If one stock is outperforming another one, the superior stock will be traded short. The stock that is not outperforming is then bought long. It is expected that this divergence will result in an increase in prices. This will enable the trader to shield the risk of the market from any changes that could render the strategy non-neutral. The risk in the market is contingent on the amount of capital you put into any stock. It also depends on stocks vulnerable to these risk factors.

Momentum-Based Strategies

Let's suppose that there is a particular market trend and, you are an algorithmic trading expert you would like to follow this trend. The prices on the market always drop over the course of the week. These statistics can be used to determine if the trend will persist or if there will be changes in the next weeks. You are able to alter your strategy or tactic in response to the decision. Then, you can decide to base your strategy for trading on the market trends you identify from these numbers. The momentum-based approach is built on these trends and the way you monitor them. You can incorporate this kind of strategy into your trading algorithm.

Strategy Paradigms

A strategy that is based on momentum will enable investors to make money from a current trend. You could also profit of these fluctuations on the marketplace. That is you could always buy more at a better price and sell at a greater rate. What are the best ways to achieve this?

Momentum If you are concerned about momentum, you are able to systematically alter the results. You could benefit from other traders that base their decisions based on emotion.

Value investing when it comes to value investing, it is essential to employ long-term reversion strategies to ensure you can invest in the space in between your current value and median price for reversion.

Short-term position: When you employ this strategy, you will be able to buy short-term positions in the stock market. The positions will continue to go upwards and downwards until there is evidence of the reverse. This strategy is counterintuitive in comparison to other popular strategies.

Strategies that have proven successful over time due to the following motives:

Certain behavioral aspects influence the premium price

The strategy will take care of the risk

Why does Momentum Works?

There are many emotional mistakes and biases to behavior that traders can display, and it's because of these that momentum can fail. It's more difficult to do since trends are not able to last forever. A trend is likely to show rapid reversals, and the highest point in any particular trend is likely to eventually come with a halt. Momentum trading always comes with greater risk in comparison to other strategies for trading. These strategies aim to profit only from the volatility of markets. It is important to put in the buy and sell orders in a timely manner in order to minimize your losses. It is possible to use the appropriate methods of risk management and establish the limit of stop-loss. In the case of momentum investing, you must keep an eye on the market and employ the appropriate diversification strategies to protect your investment.

Modeling Ideas

The first thing to be aware of when using an approach based on momentum is how to recognize the price momentum. That means you have to know how trends work. Because you're already trading, you're aware that you can spot the trend of any stock by tracking it. For instance, you could take a look at stocks that are trading within 10% of their 52 week high , or search for a company whose price has fluctuated over the past 20 weeks. It is also possible to examine trends that are shorter in case you intend to invest for only an immediate period.

Strategies of various kinds

If you are looking to understand the changes in the prices of stocks, examine the earnings in order to better understand them. Any strategy that is based on earnings surprise or the past returns can allow you to profit from the market and study the way it reacts to various kinds of data.

The Price Momentum Strategy: You could make use of this strategy to benefit from the slow response to the market. It is possible to use larger range of data, such as long-term risk.

" Momentum Strategies could employ the earnings momentum strategy if you are looking to invest in earnings that are short-term.

Market Making

If you're interested in understanding what a market-making plan is we should first take a examine what a market maker is. Wikipedia defines the term market maker as "A market maker, also known as a liquidity supplier, is a firm or an individual that quotes both a purchase and sell price for the form of a commodity or financial instrument that is stored in inventory, in hopes to profit from the bid-offer spread which is also known as a turn."

Market making is a strategy for investing in stocks that aren't often traded at the stock exchange as it provides them with greater liquidity. Market making strategies can improve or increase the demand-supply ratio that any investment has. Let's consider an example. are market makers named John who purchases shares at $500 on the market, and then sells those identical stocks for $505. He assigns $505 to 500 as the quote for the big-ask on the shares. He is unable to sell the profit in cash without generating losses. Therefore even if John was to invest more and earn more return.

Strategy Paradigms

As previously mentioned, market-making techniques help increase the liquidity of stocks in particular those that aren't trading on the markets. If you're looking to determine how liquid stocks are, it is recommended to examine the spread between bid and ask as well as the volume. Any trading algorithm can profit from this transaction. Let's continue with an example like John from the previous. Because John is market maker, John can enhance the liquidity of the stock by giving prices on either the sell or buy side. He will provide a price which will permit him to gain from the bid-offer spread is mentioned. John accepts the risks of holding these instruments for which provided the price. Market strategies are most successful if it can predict future fluctuations on price, with most accuracy.

Modeling Ideas

The trade volume as well as the bid-ask spread could be combined to form the curve of cost of liquidity. The curve represents the amount that the liquidity taker has to have to pay. If the liquidity taker intends to fulfill the orders in accordance with the highest bid and price, the cost will be the same as the amount of shares multiplied by the spread between bid and ask. If the trader exceeds the price and considers getting more volume in the fee will change to be dependent on the quantity alone. It's difficult to calculate the volume of trades as it depends on the method employed by a liquidity provider. The goal should always be to find the model that is based on the volume of trade and is compatible with changes in the prices.

Market models generally are based on these principles:

The first model is the one that we will use. The method is to concentrate on the risk associated with inventory. It is built on the cost of the stock, the risk tolerance and the most preferred position in the inventory

#2 model This model is based upon the negative selection of data that can clearly distinguish between an educated and an amateur trader. A novice trader or a noise trader has no notion of how the market works however an informed trader is equipped with the needed details. If the perception of the liquidity investor is that it's short-term, this model is designed to assist the investor to make an immediate profit. This model makes use of its statistical advantage to earn an income. If an investor is taking the long-term perspective The goal for this approach is to cut down the expense of transaction.

Machine Learning In Trading

If you are using the machine-learning approach to trading you are able to create algorithms that can determine the range of any immediate price movement within a certain interval. The benefit of this technique is that humans create the software initially, however the artificial intelligence of the system will create or expand on the software. Many stocks are based on computer models that data scientists and quants develop. These are considered to be static stocks and their price does not fluctuate according to market conditions. Machine learning models analyse large amounts of data. Machine learning models continuously improve themselves by analyzing.

Modeling

Bayesian networks which are a type used in machine-learning, in order to build models that are able to identify trends in the market. You'll need several machines to accomplish this. A system that incorporates both the evolutionary and deep-learning algorithms may be applied to more than 100 machines for the following:

Design random and massive quantities of strategies and compare those strategies with the historical data

Select the most effective strategy , and then use that pattern or style to design new strategies.

This process continues until the system is able to function completely independently.

Chapter 4: Tools Used For Algorithmic Trading

In the last 10 years the popularity of algorithmic trading has grown to enormous popularity. A lot of investors are using algorithmic trading in their investment decision. As there has been an rise in the usage of algorithmic trading, a variety of tools and services have been created. These tools are employed to trade or examine the algorithms utilized for trading. In this article we will examine nine different tools that you could employ to test the algorithm.

Web Services

You can utilize the below services if you just wish to do business through the internet using a browser. If you choose to use these tools, you do not need to worry about installing the software within your system. If you're new to the area of algorithmic trading These are the most effective tools you can use.

Quantopian

Quantopian is a hedge fund based in Boston. It is a crowdsourced service that lets you test your strategies. It allows you to backtest every algorithm you want to implement to trade. The algorithms that are built into this platform are developed in Python which means that these algorithms can only be utilized on systems with

Python installed. If you are testing this algorithm, you may perform a complete or a quick backtest based on the data you're testing. The tool will provide you with an idea of the efficiency that the algorithm has. Quantopian has a group of programmers who are working to address any problems with the algorithm. They also are working on the development of new algorithms that can improve their trading processes. The community of developers holds every day a contest where the top ten winners receive cash prizes of $5,000. If the company finds an algorithm that is successful it will award the algorithm with capital.

QuantConnect

It is also a platform where there is an IDE that you can use to test algorithms as well as live trade. It is designed with the programming technology C#, and the users are able to examine algorithms in various languages, like Java as well as Python. There's a massive global community of users and the platform gives access to crypto, forex as well as equity and futures trading. Live trading is available with other platforms , such as InteractiveBrokers, GDAX, and OANDA.

QuantRocket

The tool is able to provide live trading as well as backtesting with Interactive Brokers as the platform. It is possible to trade on US equity and on the forex market with this tool. This platform was developed exclusively for trading on Interactive Brokers. The platform however not completely available for free. There is a monthly and annual subscription to join. This platform works with different search engines too.

The LiveTrading engine and the Backtesting engines

If you are willing to put in some effort to identify the best tools to employ to build your own algorithmic trading system that can work amazing. After you have built this software then the software can be tested with the tools listed below.

Zipline-Live or Zipline

It is the Quantopian IDE is designed by using the backend of Zipline. It is an open source engine used to backtest. This program is a system-wide application that is able to be set up to run on Docker containers as well as virtual environments. Quantopian and Zipline offer the same functionality however the latter one doesn't have any data to utilize. You'll need to create your own data that you will be able to test the algorithms back on. You can also use the data zipline offers through other test back-tests. In 2017, Zipline eliminated the live trading feature however there's another tool called Zipline-Live which was created. This tool is compatible in conjunction with Interactive Brokers and has the identical features as Zipline.

BackTrader

BackTrader is among the most well-known tools that is used to test any algorithmic trading strategy you design. The tool was created by using Python and is easy to use, effective, and clear. The interface is based on the system , which means it does not have a web interface. Be aware that this program does not contain any information that you can access, however it is possible to add information to the system by using the CSV file or any other format. In the fifth version that the application was able to live trade. The majority of algorithmic traders opt to use this software to backtest their trading strategies.

IBPy

IBPy is an Python wrapper, which is utilized within the interactive broker workstation. It is a third party wrapper that is not affiliated with Interactive Broker. Prior to when Interactive Broker developed the API library with Python it was the only way to integrate with various methods written with Python. In the present, IB has released an SDK for Python but the library is no longer in use since it's not suitable for the most recent editions of Python. There are still a variety of live trading engines and tools which can be used with this library. If you're just beginning to learn the library is an excellent starting point. It is also a good idea to know about the Python SDK that IB has released. If you're looking for something less complicated, you must utilize this Alpaca Trade API Python SDK.

Analytical Tools

When you have developed an algorithmic trading system and you are ready to evaluate the software. To accomplish this, you'll have to utilize a substantial amount in raw information. Certain IDEs offer basic analysis and visualisation. Additionally, you can get details about the effectiveness of the algorithmic. You can utilize the below tools to conduct a deeper analysis.

Pyfolio

Pyfolio is a different tool developed by Quantopian. This is an open source tool that analyzes portfolios. Pyfolio is unique because it permits you to add certain levels of uncertainty to diverse information points. You can also analyze Bayesian metrics within your portfolio. This API gives you a range of visualisation tools as well as charts and these are available on the GitHub repository.

Alphalens

Alphalens is a different analytical tool acquired from Quantopian. The application differs from Pyfolio in that it can work when working with data that is raw, too. The tool is not designed for evaluating the portfolio by itself however, it can be used for predictive analysis. There are a variety of variables to perform this type of analysis. There are a variety of visualizations are available on the GitHub repository.

TradingView

TradingView is an example of a visualisation tool. The tool is free and has a user community which is always ready to assist. As this is a web-based tool that allows you to connect to various websites to get the data you input. It is possible to visualize what you've performed over the last few months or weeks in the market with this application. The tool, similar to Quantopian allows users to share their visualization and findings to other customers. You can also request feedback if you'd like.

Broker-Dealers and Execution Platforms

Interactive Brokers

If you're a trader, then you must think about using this platform. It can be described as an online broker dealer that was first introduced in 1978. The primary focus of the platform is not trading on algorithms, but it has multiple engines that allow traders to trade on the market in a timely manner. This is among the top platforms to think about.

Alpaca

The last but not least is Alpaca. The company was established in the year of 2015. This tool is free of commission which was created exclusively for trading algorithms. It also comes with an API that allows traders to trade directly with other open-source software such as MarketStore which will enable you to improve the efficiency of the financial data in time series that are stored in the database. You can use MarketStore to determine the variables that you need to consider when you'd like to place your trades.

Miscellaneous Tools

In addition to these tools and services You should also take a take a look at these tools:

Multicharts program is a specialized trading platform for forex and equities.

Enygma catalyst: This software is used primarily to trade crypto

The Qtpylib tool may employ this tool if are looking to test an algorithm with Python. We will explore an additional example later in the book.

MetaTrader The application can be used this app for live trading as well as backtesting.

The WealthLab program is a backtesting tool the application, and the language that is used is C#

I hope that this list of tools will give some ideas of the tools you can utilize to create your own algorithmic trading software. You can use these tools and play using them as you work in developing an algorithmic trading software. You can also test it.

Chapter 5: Trend Strategies

A trend trader is likely to search for ways to earn profits and to separate gains from trends. It is possible to do this by a variety of methods however there isn't a single indicator that can be used to punch the right note to make money. It is always important to take into consideration other factors , such as risk management and psychology in trading. Certain aspects, however, have made an impact. In this chapter, we will examine some strategies and guidelines that you can employ in the event that you decide to utilize trend-based strategies when trading. You can modify these strategies according to your preference or needs.

Moving Averages

Moving averages produce an uniform trend line which is based on price information. This line is an average of price for the company over a time. An investor can pick the moving average line based on the time period they wish to invest. Certain long-term trend watchers and investors select the 50-day and 100-day and 200-day moving averages. It is possible to use a moving average in many ways. The most common method is to consider the angle the moving average is moving. If the average is moving horizontally for a long time and the price is not ranging but not moving in a trend. When the angle of the moving average is upwards it means that the stock is in the upward direction. Moving averages are used to determine what the stock is doing. It cannot forecast the price over the course of a time. The crossover is the next option to make use of the moving average. When you show the 50-day and 100-day average in the graph the algorithm will issue an alert to buy in the event that the averages cross each other, in the case that the 50-day line will be above that of the line for 100 days. If not an sell signal will take place. In the event that the stock price falls higher than the moving average and the algorithm is able to place an order to buy; however, if it is below the moving average it will issue an order to sell. The value of a share is more volatile when compared with the moving average line. This is the reason that this technique can give false signals. A moving average may provide some kind of support or resistance to the price of stocks.

MACD (Moving Average Convergence Divergence)

The divergence of convergence in the moving average is an indicator that oscillates. The values change between zero and values greater than zero. It is a trend-following and momentum indicator. One of the most simple methods of reading MACD is to read the MACD is to take a look at the histogram and determine which lines are. When the MACD lines have been higher than zero for some time then the trend is most likely to continue to grow. When you notice that the MACD line is lower than zero a period of time, the trend will be downward. The algorithm will put an order to buy whenever the MACD moves above the zero line and put a sell order in the event of a decline. The algorithm is able to use signals lines to make an order to buy or sell. The two lines on an MACD graph: two lines - a fast and slow one. If your fast line lies over the slower line and it crosses that line the algorithm will issue an buy signal. In the other case it will issue the signal to sell.

RSI (Relative Strength Index)

It is an additional indicator that fluctuates. Because it's value is between between zero and 100, it is a more reliable indicator contrasted with the MACD. One method to look at an RSI is to consider the price as a higher rate that needs to be corrected. When the histogram indicator is higher than 70, it's believed to be that the value of the share is being oversold. It is time to change in the event that the indicator is lower than 30. When the price is rising then the price of the stock could rise to 70 and could exceed it if it continues to increase in price. A downtrend can push prices of the stock down to 30 or less. The overbought or oversold price for a stock is an accurate method to determine the value of shares. In addition, traders can opt to purchase an overbought stock or share in times of rising trend. Let's assume that the stock is on the market in the long term, and that its trend is up. If the RSI for the stock is lower than 50, your system will put a buy order on the stock. This indicates that there's an increase in the value of that stock. The trader will buy the stock after this pullback is over and the trend will continue. The RSI value is 50 because it will not fall to 30 unless there's a downward trend. A trendline or a moving average is a way to define the direction that the signal for trading will be moving.

On-Balance-Volume (OBV)

The most important indicators is the volume. With this strategy you'll be looking at a huge amount of data and then combine the details into data which shows the only indicator. This indicator is able to gauge the amount of pressure that is put on selling and buying. It is achieved through adding up the volumes of a stock during days when price is rising and subtracting the volume when it is lower. It is possible to use the volume to verify any patterns with regard to the cost of the share. The price that is rising is correlated with a rising OBV and a decrease in price is connected to an eroding OBV. If the OBV increases, however the price doesn't rise, it is likely to increase in a sudden manner and rise to the OBV. However when the price increases but the OBV drops or is flat, the value that the company is near to the top. However, should the reverse occur, the price would be getting close to the bottom.

Conclusion

Indicators can be used to simplify the information about prices. They can also be used to warn you in the event of a reversal or to provide signals for trading trends. A indicator is comprised of a number of variables that you can alter to your personal preferences. The indicators are able to be used across all time periods. You may also mix different indicators strategies or establish your own rules. It is important to define the criteria for entry and exit before you start trading. The indicator can be utilized in a variety of ways. If you are planning to use one particular indicator it is recommended to conduct additional investigation and try it out before you make use of it on the market. It is difficult to master to trade using indicators. If you've never had the opportunity to trade before, it is important to be aware of the meaning of a brokerage account. The only method to access the market of stocks.

Chapter 6: Skills Needed

If you're interested in being an algorithmic trading trader you must possess the following essential skills:

1. Programming skills

2. Risk Management skills

3. Statistics skills

These are skills that are considered essential abilities. In addition to these abilities you must also be aware of large data analytics, machine intelligence as well as numerical optimization. These aren't huge tools , but they can be extremely powerful. They can aid in making your trading experience easy. Additionally, you can make use of macroeconomics, microstructure of markets as well as behavioral finance, to help get a better understanding of the market and gain greater insight. These aren't a required necessity, but they will assist you in forming the best concepts to help you develop the most effective strategy.

Overview

The skills discussed in this article are fundamental skills you require to acquire if you wish to be trader. Let's examine how these skills can assist you in becoming an automated trader.

Programming

It is essential to master code if you are planning to be the algorithmic trading. This will enable you to complete the necessary research. It is essential to be proficient in the languages of C++ and Java. It is also important to know about various data structure fundamentals and algorithms. It is only through this that to ensure that you can have a solid base. Nowadays, the language which is utilized for the algorithmic trade is Python. If you are willing to put in the effort and practice, you'll be fluent in this language.

It's also a great idea to master some advanced programming languages, such as R as well as Python. Python is a simple to master and is an excellent tool to collect and manage, gather and clean data from a variety of sources. It is possible to use Python as an instrument to conduct research because this language makes it simpler to analyze data. There are several useful libraries available in Python that you can make use of such as NumPy or Pandas.

You can also utilize R to conduct some analysis and research. The language is a huge repository that includes a number of applications and library. R was the first language to be written to be used exclusively for statistical analysis. It is utilized by algorithmic traders for the necessary analysis. If you're engineering, then you may select to use MATLAB because it is extremely beneficial. You may choose to study one of these languages at a high level, but not all. We'll go over some details on Python in the next chapter. There are many cross-platform capabilities within these high-level programming languages you can determine which language is most suitable for your needs.

Simulation

After you've learned write code, then you will be able to take on different modeling tasks. You can write code in the language you already know. Then, run the simulation to allow the test of your programming skills for the use algorithms for trading. It is also possible to use other simulations that have been developed by others prior to composing your simulation writing. The flexibility, speed and precision are the most important factors to take into consideration when developing in a plan. Simulations can assist you by assisting you in conducting real-time research and create the most effective strategies for trading.

Statistics

You need to have some understanding of statistics if you are looking to succeed being an algorithmic trader. Be aware that statistics are the foundation of all you do. It is essential to think about statistics when developing strategies, plan risk management, evaluate the effectiveness of the strategy, or choose the best strategy to use. It is essential to know the statistical concepts if you wish to test your ideas for algorithmic trading. Regression analysis can be used to test as well as correlations and other tests based on statistics. These tests can be used to examine the strategy's underlying principles and how it can work to adapt to fluctuations in markets. By using statistics, you will be able to give an insight into how each action can be more than the risk involved with the trade.

Risk Management

It is crucial to take into consideration the possibility of risk when working with an algorithmic trading expert. A variety of risk factors become apparent when you consider an algorithmic trade process. For example, counterparty risk as well as risk of trade, portfolio risk and risk to infrastructure are all considered to be component of the process.

Other risks could be present such as servers being shut down or interruption of the power or network. There are other risks that could include the broker becoming into bankruptcy, or losing the trading accounts you have, and many more. This is a tricky subject that requires you to be aware of the various risks you could face. It is essential to understand about both Kelly Allocation and Mean Variance Optimization.

It's always beneficial to think of concepts for yourself. Avoid using the ideas of someone else constantly. If you are able to conduct rigorous and objective research, you can accomplish this effortlessly. You need to create practical applications. That is how to use what you've read. It is possible to increase your skills to succeed in the field of algorithmic trading. If you put the strategies that you have learned into practice then your abilities will grow. If you decide to concentrate on a particular area you may break it down into smaller parts so you are able to master the skill. For instance, if , for example, you begin to learn Python then you must break down the task into understanding the kinds of data, the conditional statement loops and variables, functions, debugging, and much more. It is possible to break down each of these tasks into smaller ones when needed.

This is the best method to master any task efficiently.

Chapter 7: The Introduction Of Python

Installing and Running Python

Python is a program or tool that you are able to install and run on various operating systems like Linux, Unix, Windows as well as Mac OS X or OS/2. The majority of systems are now equipped with Python particularly those running Mac OS X and Linux systems. The experts say this is the most effective method to use Python since it's already installed on the system. There is no need to install the language, and then verifying that it functions properly. If your computer does not include it then you must follow the directions in the next sections.

Installing on Windows

First, you must download Python after which you need to make modifications to the settings to ensure that the software is compatible with your operating system. It is essential to do this prior to using the code included in the book. You must read the directions to follow them phrase by word while you are changing your operating system. The following links can aid you in the process:

http://www.Python.org/doc/faq/windows/

http://wiki.Python.org/moin/BeginnersGuide/Download

http://docs.Python.org/dev/3.0/using/windows.html

It is recommended to install the latest officially-licensed Python installer. Alternate versions for Itanium or AMD machines. You can download these using the following link: http://www.Python.org/download/. This file, with an .msi extension, must be saved in a suitable place. After the installation wizard has started and you are ready to allow the installation process to continue. Make sure to use the suggested settings until you are aware of the changes you have to make.

Installing on other Systems

Python is also able to be installed on different systems. You can follow the directions to install Python for Linux and Unix similar systems by visiting the following websites:

http://docs.Python.org/dev/3.0/using/unix.html

If you're using OS X, follow the instructions listed in the following paragraphs:

http://www.Python.org/download/mac/

http://docs.Python.org/dev/3.0/using/mac.html

How do you choose the right Version?

Different versions of Python have different numbers after Python These numbers are a reference to what version numbers are used. If you go through the archives of multiple websites, the number of versions will vary between 2.5.2 to 3.0 The former is an older but still usable version of Python and the latter is the most recent version. The Python team launched version 2.6 in the same year that it launched version 3.0. A few programmers are still using the 2.6 version due to being familiar with the API but they still want to utilize new features the language can offer.

This language is continuously evolving The current version is 3.7.4. Keep in mind that these versions are identical to version 3.0 however, there are certain improvements. So, the latest versions will be called 3.0 in this guide.

Python can run in different ways across different platforms and you'll need to understand how to use it with your particular system, using the instructions provided by the API. The examples of algorithmic trade code are able to function in the same way across every operating system. If you want to know more about Python it is recommended to study the documentation created by the developers. They is available for free and well written. It is available at http://www.Python.org/doc/. Because Python is a language that is easy to master, traders prefer to make use of it when creating code to build the trading programs they use.

Getting Started

If you are planning to create an algorithmic trading system, you must first define the issue. Find out what you'd like to achieve prior to writing the program. Consider the strategy you would like to use in addition. This will allow you to develop an accurate idea of how you'd like to tackle the issue.

In the coming chapters, we'll explore how you can compose code with Python. We will explore the most crucial features in Python in order to assist you master the language more efficiently. Keep in mind that the information provided in this book isn't comprehensive. It is important to go through the manual to gain a deeper understanding of the language. These steps can help you improve your understanding of the language, and will help you develop your thoughts into computer software.

Chapter 8: Variables And Data Types

This section will explain the different kinds of variables you can utilize when writing programs using Python. We will also discuss how to transform your ideas into working program with Python. It's only after you are able to comprehend how variables work and what data type you are using that you are able to begin programming. The examples provided in this section will make it easier for you to understand how to make use of variables and data types in your programming.

The programs described above can be easily written using multiple variables. When using variables, you are able to specify the function, method or calculation to be applied to find a solution without knowing the type of value the variable should refer to prior to. Every bit of data that is put into a system has to be converted into variables before it is used in the context of a function. This output can be only received when these variables are utilized by functions as parameter.

Python Keywords

Every programming language comes with an alphabet of keywords which form the basis for the programming language. The same is true for the Python language, too. It is not possible to use these words for naming an identifier, or variable in your program as these are the essential words of the language. If you are using these terms in your code, but do not spell them correctly the interpreter will give an error. Let's look at a few of the terms we will be using in the following chapters:

False

None

Assert

True

As

Break

Continue

#Def

Import

In

Is

And

Class

Del

For

From

Global

Raise

Return

Else

Elif

Not

Or

Pass

Other than

#Try

While

With

Final

If

Lambda

Non-local

Yield

Knowing the Naming Convention

Let's examine the words you can use. It is possible to use different names for variables. However, each variable should start by using an underscore, or letter. Certain variables can include numbers, however they can't begin with one. If the interpreter encounters the variables which start with a number rather than quotation marks or letters that it will treat the variable as a numerical. It is not recommended to make use of any other type of underscore or number to indicate a variable within your program. Because Python is a language that takes into account case It is imperative that you use the same name throughout the whole program. For instance, the words variables1 and Variable1 can be two distinct variables, as per the interpreter.

Incorporating Values and Creating Variables Variables

Variables can be created using the following steps:

1. The initialization phase is the point where you identify the variable and assign a type of data to the variable. You must attach the label on it.

2. Assignment: You'll assign the variable a value at this point.

This process is performed with only one command in Python with the equal sign. If you need to assign an amount to a number, you need to create this code in the form:

Variable = value

Every part of code that executes one function, such as the assignment of a task, can be known as an expression. The expression is the portion in the program that the executor or compiler can analyze. Let's take a an example:

Length = 14

Breadth = 10

Height = 10

Area_Triangle = Length * Breadth * Height

Any variable is able to be assigned a number or an expression, such as the assignment for Area_Triangle in the above example.

Every statement has to be written in a distinct line. If you write the statement down in the same manner as you note down a shopping list then you're doing it the correct way. Each recipe starts the same manner with the ingredients listed and the quantities and equipment you'll require to prepare the dish. Similar to when you write Python program - you begin by defining the variables you intend to utilize and then develop methods and functions to apply with the variables.

Recognizing Different Variables of Different Types

The Python interpreter recognizes various types of variables: lists or sequences words, numbers, or String literals Booleans or mappings. These variables are frequently employed in Python applications. A variable called None has its own name, which is called NoneType. Before we examine how numbers and words are utilized in Python first, we need to examine the typing capabilities in Python.

Working using Dynamic Typing

If the assign value an object the interpreter is able the kind of value that the variable has, also known as dynamic typing. This type of typing doesn't affect the speed at which you type on your keyboard. As opposed to other languages Python doesn't require the user declare the kinds of variables that are used in the program. This could be viewed as positive and negative. The benefit is that you don't have to be concerned about the type of the variable as you write the code and you just need to be concerned about how it behaves.

Dynamic typing in Python allows the interpreter to deal with the unpredictable input of users. The interpreter that runs Python accepts various forms of input from the user. To these, the interpreter assigns an evolving type meaning that a single line of code is able to handle words, numbers or any other type of data. The user doesn't always have to be aware of what data type the variable has to be. Because you don't have to declare a variable using Python prior to using it, you could be enticed to add the variable elsewhere in your code. Be aware that you'll never get any error message from Python when you create the variable which does not have an associated value. However, it is quite easy for programmers to get lost of the variables that are utilized and the locations where they are created within the script. You may choose to carry out two distinct tasks when you wish to avoid these problems. It is necessary to employ these strategies, especially when you are beginning to create multiple variables within your script. One option is to bundle all variables together at the beginning of your code. It is also possible to assign standard values for these variables. The other option is to keep a record of the various variables that you have created.

This can be accomplished by keeping a data table in the comments or in the documents you write for each program.

Python must always keep track of variables you add to the script. The first reason is that the computer will have to store some memory in order to store the value of the variable. It is essential to note that every type of data requires different amounts of space. Another reason is that if you are aware of the various variables, you'll be able to be sure to avoid mistakes within your program. Python will report an error referred to as TypeError when you use the wrong variable. support the operation. It may be a bit annoying initially, but it is among the most useful aspects that Python has to offer. Let's take a look at an following example:

>>3.

>>C = word

>>trace = false

>>>

B + c

Traceback (most recent call, last):

File "" Line 1 File ", line 1

TypeError: Operand not supported type(s) to + int and str'

>>> C - - trace

Traceback (most recent call, last):

File "" line 1 File ", line 1

TypeError: Operand not supported type(s) that include - "str" and "bool."

The above program tries to use data types that are not compatible. It is not possible to eliminate the Boolean answer, or include any number into the text variable. It is imperative to change the type of data prior to you attempt to use it. It is essential to convert the data type into another one that is compatible to the process. You can mix words and numbers in the same way normal, but you can't do arithmetic operations with a text data type. Python will issue an alert, known as the TypeError. It can assist you in locating the problem in the script that you wrote. The error will reveal where the error occurs within the code and direct you to the specific line. Then, you can make sure that you give your code clear directions to ensure that you are able to extract the correct value in the calculation.

A data type is utilized to help you represent information that is available on the ground. What I mean by real world is the one which is not a computer. In the earlier examples we utilized the data types str and int. It is soon clear that these types of data are only utilized to identify the most basic information.

It is possible to combine these types of data to create complicated data types. We will discuss this further within the text. It is first necessary to know more about the building blocks you can use to define your data, and as well, identify the sequence of actions you'd like to take to alter the data held within these variables.

The None Variable

A predefined variable named None is a particular number in Python. It is a valuable variable and can be helpful in situations where you have to create a new variable but do not specify or define an amount to the variable. If you assign values, such as "" and"0," the interpreter will identify the variable as str or int variable.

Information = No

A variable may be assigned the value None by using the previous statement. The following examples make use of real-world data which can be transformed into a virtual representation by using some fictional characters. This example employs some stats to illustrate some of the characteristics of the characters, to provide information to fighting system. This example can be used to streamline your database and your accounts. Let's look at the time to look at some of the characters used in the sample.

The program that you used, hello_world.py, you saw the way to create a basic output by using printing () method. This function is able to print values for variables as well as the literal sequence of letters. In most cases, every print statement should begin on a new line, however several variables can print on the same line by using a space to divide the variables. Print () to join all variables onto one line, with spaces.

"Goblin," "Goblin, "Goblin"

Genre = "Female"

>>> print (Gender, Race)

Female Goblin

Different parts of data are able to be put together into one line by using a variety of methods. Certain methods are more efficient as compared to other methods. Strings that are adjacent but not separated will be automatically concatenated however this isn't an option that is applicable to all variables.

>>Print ("Male" "Elf")

The above expression will result in the output below - "MaleElf"

If you type in the code below,

>>> > print ("Male" Print ("Male")

The following error message:

File " " Line 1

Print ("Male" race)

^

SyntaxError incorrect syntax

This method is not suitable because you can't create a string function using variables and string as a string since it's simply a method of writing one line of string.

Utilizing Quotes

In Python the word "character" is used to refer to one number, punctuation mark or an individual letter. The string or characters that is used to display text is referred to as strings or string literals. If you must inform the interpreter that you wish to display the text block to be displayed in text, you should wrap the characters with quotation marks. This syntax may take a variety of forms , including

A text string enclosed in only single quotation marks.'

"A Text string that is enclosed with two quotes."

" A text sting that is enclosed in three quote marks .'''

In the event that the wording is placed within quotes this is considered to be as str (string).

Nesting Quotes

There are instances that you'll need to use quotation marks that are literal within your code. Python lets you include the quotation marks within another group of quotation marks when you are using a different kind or quotation marks.

Texttext "You are learning to' make use of nesting quotation marks in Python."

In the above example the interpreter will conclude that it is at its end once it is at its end string at the second double quote in the string preceding. So the substring 'how" is considered to be a component of the principal string with the quote marks. This way you will have at the very least an upper level of quotation marks. The easiest method to learn how to use nested quotes is to play with different kinds of strings.

>>> > boilerplate """

... #===(")===#===(*)===#===(")===#

... ARG

... Version '0.1'

... "FiliBuster" technology inc.

... #===(")===#===(*)===#===(")===#

... """

>>> print(boilerplate) #=== (") ===#=== (*) ===#=== (") ===#

Egregious Response Generator

Version '0.1'

"FiliBuster" technologies inc.

#===(")===#===(*)===#===(")===#

This is a good technique to employ when you need to format an entire block of text or even a complete page.

How do you use whitespace characters?

Whitespace characters can be distinguished when the sequence of characters starts with an 'n. "n" is the linefeed character different from the 'r character. The output screen the former will shift out to the next line and the latter shifts the output into an entirely new paragraph. It is important to understand the differences between the different operating systems convert the output.

The meaning and usage of certain sequences is lost on a lot of instances. It is common to use n to move to the next line. Another helpful sequence is t which is used to create an indentation on text by creating tab characters. The majority of others whitespace symbols are employed only in certain instances.

Sequence Its Meaning

New line

The Return of Carriage

t Tab

V Vertical Tab

\e Escape Character

f Formfeed

b Backspace

A Bell

You can follow the following example to create the output you want to display on your screen:

>>> print ("Characters\n\nDescription\nChoose your character\n \

.... \tDobby\n\tElf\n\tMale\nDon\'t forget to escape \'\\\\\'."

)

Characters

Description

Select your character

Dobby

Elf

Male

Do not forget to get out of the way. '\.'

It is important to remember it is immutable for strings meaning that they can't be altered. It is also possible to use simple methods in order to make new strings using different values.

Converting Data Types

There are a variety of built-in functions by Python to convert values from one type of data into another. The types of data that are commonly used include:

Int (x) can be can be used for converting any number to an integer

floating (x) can be used to convert numbers to a data type float

str (object) Convert any type of string into strings which can be used to print.

```
>>> Float (23)

23.0

>>> Int (23.5)

23

>>> >>> (int (23.5))

23
```

The Right Identifier

Each line of code is identified by an identifier. The editor or compiler in Python will look at every word which is surrounded using quotation marks hasn't had a comment or escapes in a manner that it is not identified as an identifyr. Because an identifier is an identifier that could mean almost anything. It is therefore sensible to use names that will be recognized to the target language. It is important to choose a name which is not utilized in the code currently for identifying any variable that is new.

If you select an identity that is identical to the name of the previous the original variable will become unaccessible. This might be unwise when the name is chosen as a key element in your code. Fortunately, when writing an application in Python the language doesn't permit you to create a variable that has the same name that has been used before. The next section in this chapter lists the most important words, sometimes known as keywords in Python that will assist you in avoiding this problem.

Chapter 9: What You Need To Do Be An Algo Trader Pro

Expertise of Algorithmic trading

In order to be successful Algorithmic trader, you have to have a set of abilities that allow you to compete on the market, but also offer you the profit you want. Algo trading involves the use of automated purchase and sale transactions that involve financial instruments such as bonds, stocks and futures. You must have an electronic networked connection with buy and sell companies as well as brokers and a platform for the selling and buying as along with other tasks in trading like monitoring the market's vulnerability and price fluctuations.

In order to accomplish this it is necessary to possess an array of abilities which make it easier for you to accomplish these tasks.

Technical Skills

The algorithmic trading industry requires the user to possess two kinds of technical expertise that are domain knowledge and development of code. Domain knowledge is about understanding the trends in stocks across various industries. In contrast programming skills require you to have a good grasp of programming languages.

Numbers as well as Numbers

Any potential Algorithmic trader must be proficient in math in addition to quantitative analysis. For example, if terms like skewness, the conditional probability, or kurtosis aren't a mystery to the person who is reading this, then you are a long way from become an Algorithmic trader.

An in-depth understanding of mathematics is vital since you must conduct study, validate the results and come up with trading strategies. Knowing mathematics is essential as it allows you to develop strategies that are foolproof. As trade executions become speedier and efficient it is important to ensure that you are aware of all the details about numbers. Make sure you are aware that a minor error in the code that is used to create it could result in huge trading loss.

Core Skills

Additionally, you must possess at minimum three essential technical abilities including risk management, programming and statistics. These are not the only basic capabilities you require. In addition to the essential capabilities, you'll also need big analysis of data as well as numerical optimization as well as machine-learning. They may not be as crucial than the fundamental capabilities, but they're nevertheless effective enough to make trading more smooth.

Economic and Financial Knowledge

Understanding behavioral microstructure of markets, finance and macroeconomics can help you make important choices and make sense of the market more. Although they aren't an element of the minimum requirements, they can help in making trading decisions which ultimately affect the results on your trading.

A Review of Core Technical Skills

Let's explore how the basic technical abilities can help you reach your Algorithmic trading objectives.

Programming

You should be acquainted with data mining, analysis research, using automated trading platforms.

Understanding programming is crucial because it lets you do research. Learn two or three C-based languages like C++ or Java. Therefore, you should be more focused upon data structures as well as Algorithms which provide you with an understanding of trading.

For greater research, it's recommended that you get familiar with a programming language that is higher-level like Python, R, or MATLAB. These languages are simple to master as long as you have the appropriate platform. The most used language is Python. It is crucial to understand the language as it will help to collect data, process it and organize it from various sources. It's also an excellent instrument for conducting research as it allows users to perform analytics on data thanks to the many libraries that can be used for this task.

In the same way, you can go for R for research and data analysis since it's backed by a massive collection of libraries and functions. R was designed with the idea of statistical analysis in mind, and is an ideal match for the type of work required from traders. Algorithmic trader.

If you're a little knowledgeable of engineering, MATLAB is the best choice.

You are able to choose any of these languages, but it's not important to learn all of them since most of them have the ability to cross-pollinate. As time passes, you will come to understand which language is best suited for your requirements.

Experience with spreadsheets and other concepts like the structuring of data and large data is an advantage.

Speed Accuracy, Speed, and Flexibility

These are the skills are required to acquire so that you can complete your work efficiently and quickly. To improve these skills it is essential to perform modelling tasks in the simulation environment. The simulation environment provides the ability to test various tasks you're planning to complete.

You may choose to have your own simulation system or utilize simulations created through other trading professionals. Simulation allows you to build and improve these skills in order to create trading strategies, as well as conduct actual research.

Statistics Knowledge

A solid understanding of statistics is essential for anyone Algorithmic trader who wants to succeed. Statistics are at the core of every task you have to deal in your trades, all the way from performance evaluation to risk management and the development of strategies to make decisions.

Statistics are the basis of the majority the Algorithmic trading concepts. Some of the statistical applications you'll use include the use of statistical tests, correlations as well as regression analyses.

In this case, you can use statistical analysis to decide if the market you're in at a specific time is suitable to trade in or not. Regression analysis can also be used to test the validity of analysis to test ideas related to various aspects that impact the market.

Risk Management

This is an essential job for every Algorithmic trader. When you place orders in markets of any kind, traders are confronted with diverse risk factors like infrastructure risk, counterparty risk, and many other risk factors that can occur at the both the trade and portfolio levels. The risks you face can take a variety of forms like the possibility of your servers being shut down due to a variety of causes, or the loss from your trade account if an intermediary goes bankrupt as well as the failure of a counter-party to finish an order.

To minimize the risk it is essential to comprehend the basic principles for risk-management. It is a complicated area which requires you to comprehend the options available to limit the risks. To accomplish this, be sure to learn about the concepts of Mean-Variance Optimization along with Kelly Allocation.

Test of ideas

For traders One of the strategies you must have is progress. It is essential to progress between one step to the next. In order to do this you must develop habits of testing the ideas you have, rather than relying on concepts that have been tried through other dealers. In order to test the ideas you have, it is necessary to conduct high-quality and objective research.

The research process helps you decide what you need to do to reach your objectives. It is also important to think of practical ways to implement them. Research will allow you to comprehend the current trends on the market for trading and also how you can incorporate them into your trading strategies.

Implementing the concepts you've learned it will help you improve your technical abilities and create a mental model and imagination that will help you successful in Algorithmic trading.

To acquire the various abilities It is essential that you assign sub-tasks each to help you are able to master it more effectively. For example, when learning Python programming It is essential to divide it into various subtasks which comprise loops, data types variables, syntax familiarity, operations, troubleshooting, as well as objects-oriented programming. It is also possible to subdivide the subtasks into smaller assignments to make learning easier.

Be aware of common trading concepts

You will need to find and create your own unique trading strategies and models entirely from scratch. Also, you need the skills to modify established models. You must be familiar with some of the most successful trading strategies.

Computer Use

If you are you are an Algorithmic trader, you'll have to execute your trades with real-time data that includes quotations and prices for commodities. This means that you have to be acquainted with the systems, specifically terminals that supply data feeds and content. Additionally, you must be comfortable using charting and analysis software and also be able to utilize brokers trading platforms to find and execute orders.

Soft Skills

As trader, you must have the right skills to be successful on the market.

The first step is to adopt the right attitude. Be aware that not all people can behave as a trader. The most successful traders are always seeking out innovative ways to handle trades. They are able to adjust to ever-changing market and thrive under pressure due to the long working hours.

Second, you have to be willing to fail. Certain trading strategies may appear to be foolproof, but once you test them and find that they're not exactly what you expected. Many hopeful traders fail because they trust in the concept and attempt to force it to perform regardless of the fact that market conditions aren't in their favor. They are unable to admit failure and are unwilling to abandon the notion they've taken on. In contrast successful traders are able to tell that an idea doesn't work and then explore a different strategy.

Thirdly, you have to develop an innovative mind. The market is constantly evolving day-in and day-out so the idea you are implementing won't be profitable over an extended period of time. Since different systems compete against each and each other, it's up to you to choose what is best for you and which won't be beneficial to you. Keep in mind that the choices you make about the best method will determine whether you are able to survive or fail. That's why you need to ensure that you search for new ideas to make the most of opportunities that may soon vanish.

Financial Marketing Acumen

Before you begin to dive into the world of algo trading it is essential to know the basics of the financial market. All the statistical and programming information is useless if you aren't aware of what financial markets actually are. It is important to comprehend the various types of technology used within the market in order to understand the reasons behind why price fluctuations occurs.

Capabilities for Problem-solving

It is essential to find solutions to problems that come out of trading. There is no assurance that every trade will yield the results that you would like - sometimes, you'll fail. The skills to deal with problems help you find the best trade strategies, as in illustrating the concepts to meet your specific needs. A good problem-solving skill gives an individual the capability to think of solutions.

Data Management

Accessing reliable information is crucial for every trader. Although vendors and markets provide various kinds of information at various prices, it can be difficult to get access to historical intraday data. Therefore, it is essential to know the data patterns across all markets worldwide.

After you have your data first, it is time to cleanse it up and organize it so that it's consistent and compatible with your database. Then, you have to use the data to detect patterns, create different patterns, and then optimize them.

Know System Architecture

The majority of trading transactions occur through an online platform for trading. It is therefore essential that you know how a trading platform works and how to utilize it. You must be aware of the different components of the system like the adaptors, the event process engine and much more.

Compliance and Regulations

Each region has their own rules and regulations must be adhered to in order to for trading in the market. These rules pertain to co-location as well as the short-selling process, approval of systems and many more you'll need to be aware of.

For instance, certain exchanges require approval at the system level, whereas others require approval at the strategic level.

Simple Trading Strategies

When you have your math and programming abilities in order The next step is to get into the actual work. Making orders is about employing a particular strategy that you can rely on, discover the different strategies and the situations are used to determine the best strategy depending on the type of trade you are looking to make.

It is the Mindset that is the basis of Pro Algorithmic Trading.

The profession of a trader doesn't only consist about formulating strategies and doing the most thorough analysis of data, it's about having the right mindset. Different aspects distinguish a winning trader from one who constantly loses:

* Successful traders don't develop better strategies for trading.

* They're not any better than other traders.

They aren't able to conduct more thorough market analysis.

Only one thing distinguishes the successful trader from the losers one is the mindset that they have adopted.

Many traders make the error of thinking that all they need to do is find an excellent trading strategy. They believe that all they need to do is learn the technique, sign in to the market every day, then the marketplace will begin adding money to their account.

It's not happening as they expected. In fact, thousands of people employ smart system that is well-designed, yet they make more losses than they earn in their end.

People who are able to have money in account are the ones who have developed the ideal mentality that lets them be successful. They have certain psychological principles, beliefs and behaviors that make them ideal for overcoming the trading market.

The Attitude

Many traders, particularly the who lose they believe it is the case that markets are in fact rigged against them. This false belief affects the capacity to trade. If you take a look into the marketplace and believe it is working against you, it's time to realize that there are lots of traders who are trading with success in the same market as well.

Each market is neutral, which is why you'll see more and increasing numbers of people signing up for this and using it to manage their trades both day and night.

One of the greatest qualities that the majority of successful traders possess is self-confidence. They are convinced that they will succeed in the trades they engage in.

A lot of traders who lose However, many traders who lose are self-aware that they're cursed and that this will become a fulfilled prophecy. If you are doubtful of your capabilities it is common to be reluctant to make a move that could have turned profitable in the end. Also, they tend to cut their profits due to the belief that the market will eventually reverse its course.

The traders who are successful recognize that the market may occasionally not match their expectations, but they do not abandon their hopes that easily. They conduct analyses of market trends, yet they are aware that even the most thorough analysis may not be able to match with the market's movements. They know when is the best moment to trade, and they plan ahead to make the trade whenever the opportunity presents itself.

What are the characteristics of successful traders?

They have traits that they have:

* They take risks

The most successful traders are comfortable taking risks. People who aren't comfortable with taking risks aren't the best traders in the world. Be aware that losing is a part of trading. Investors who are looking to win are able to take the risk when trading. They realize that trading isn't the same as placing money into savings accounts in which there is a guarantee of returns.

* They Adjust to Changes quickly

Successful traders are able to adjust to the changes in the market quickly enough. Many traders who lose are unable remove themselves from the trades which once served them and so they continue to become enthralled by their market analysis. For the winners If the analysis indicates they have to alter their position on price changes, they go ahead and make the change fast.

* They are disciplined

They evaluate the market and every other aspect with a clear mind, and regardless of how the market reacts to them, they never alter their views or objectives. They follow strict rules of money management which allow them to estimate the potential risk and rewards prior to committing to any trade.

* They're Not Emotional in Their Trades

As trader, you understand how trades can be a whimper whether it's up or down. It's the direction in which you trade that decides whether you will win or lose. Successful traders don't have the moment to be overly thrilled when they make trades successful or be devastated when they lose trades. Instead, they take control of their emotions and don't let the trading events influence their lives.

Beyond the mentality that traders have, they have some behaviors that help them win constantly. They include:

* They often evaluate their performance and then review the trades after trades as well as day-after-day. They are aware the importance of trading as a process which must be developed and developed by embracing concepts that work and putting aside ones that don't work at all.

* They're adaptable. These traders don't place their personal egos into the transactions they make. They evaluate the market objectively and are willing to discard any suggestions that don't work for them.

* They are willing to take on risk when they recognize an opportunity for profit which is based on a trading strategy and analysis of the market. But, you'll notice that they do not risk their money in reckless ways. Instead they are aware of the percentage of risk as well as the percentage of return, and this determines their choices.

They know that the Market cannot be predicted.

The most successful traders realize that the market is constantly changing every day and is unpredictable. They also realize that there isn't a sure-fire method to predict price movements accurately. This is why they keep an eye out for indicators that could indicate incorrect price predictions and then re-evaluate their strategies accordingly.

A losing trader after placing an order tends to search at market movements which prove that they are correct, and minimize any market movement that appears to contradict their research. The majority of them have to lose trades, suffering a great deal of loss.

The discipline of a trader

Trading environments are free of restrictions and the market is an open environment which you can utilize to purchase and sell, as well as enter and exit at any time you like. There is no obligation to adhere to any specific rules for trading at any price or period. Because of this fat, you can take any decision you like anytime you want. It's up to you to choose the best way to proceed - either reckless or discipline.

The most effective way to approach it is to ensure you have an established set of rules that control the trading and be controlled.

Discipline is essential to win trades. However, it is difficult for the majority of people to comprehend and adhere to. A lot of people do well when they have rules that come from outside sources, instead of from within the rules themselves. A lot of people believe that since they created the rule they are free to alter the rules. While this may be feasible and is possible but it's not a winning approach.

Common Mistakes Algorithmic traders Make

One of the most important problems to be addressed as an algo trader are the mistakes you commit when trading. The most frequent mistakes are made in the trading environment or during the testing stage. Let's look at a couple of them.

Inability to recognize the differences between Short and Long Positions

A lot of times, traders does not know the difference between bearish and bullish markets, which is confusing him when taking on the positions available for sale (Short) and buying (Long).

The necessity to solely rely on technical Analysis Indicators

While conducting your research, you'll find a great deal of writing that discusses indicators. This is accompanied by numerous instances of their application in trading. They can also be used to aid in the development of trade algorithms, however the signals require to be examined and verified by applications which can calculate the result.

Inability to match the strategy to the right product or the Right Group of products or groups of

One of the most common challenges that occur when a trader is when they don't select the appropriate mix of products in trading. It is important to determine whether your strategy suitable for a different product from the one you're trading right now. By doing this, you can gain more value out of your strategy.

Overtrading

It could mean a variety of things. It could mean too much leverage, or just placing too much bet on one trade. It can also mean making too many trades, which could can harm your overall performance.

In this case you should look for ways to decrease the amount of trades. Make sure you pick a wise trade or opt for higher intervals. Instead of trading for one minute choose to go for 30-minute or longer.

System Interference

The purpose of the algorithm trader is that it handle the work. Don't think about it or what it should do, and don't alter it once it's running, or think about ways to increase the speed. Leave the system to perform as you have programmed it to work.

Over-optimization

Many traders are looking to extract more cash out of the system in the fastest time. This is a common practice even if you do not know the concept at all However, you must be able to recognize when your system is operating in an overoptimization mode.

Expecting Low Profits per Trade

Focus your strategies on a greater profits per transaction. Anything that is less than $50 is lowand you'll be struggling to pay the commissions as well as other trading expenses.

Looking for strategies that have No Exit

Be wary of strategies that don't provide a solution and especially those that do not have a system for managing money implemented.

Failure to prepare for the unexpected

In the world of algo trading, something can occur. The internet connection may be down, or the servers could crash and you could lose all the data you had operating. It is possible to encounter these and other situations you did not anticipate to be in the first place. That's why it's essential to be prepared for any eventuality!

To prevent this from happening the risk, you must put into your account only the amount you're willing to risk and ensure that you only accept a risk that your account is able to be able to bear.

This does not include Commission as well as Slippage during the backtest

A lot of traders don't include the cost of transactions in their estimations so that, when they receive the results, they realize that they're losing money since the entire profit is taken up by cost of transactions.

Overconfidence

A major mistake you must avoid when trading is overconfidence. Some novice traders may be lucky initially, but the next time they are too confident until they risk too high a risk. Keep in mind that being gentle and smart is the most important factor to a successful trading career.

Treating your trading as A Hobby

Imagine telling people that you're making money through the algo market, yet you don't have any records of your stock, sales, and more the people will think you're lying!

The same is true for you can't trade if don't have the proper documents. The use of records lets you understand the things that work and don't perform. You must record different aspects of your trade that you can keep track of, such as how much you've put into and the position you want to hold and so on.

Chapter 10: Methodologies Of Algorithmic Trading

There are many strategies of Algorithmic trading you could choose to use to earn an income. Let's take a examine each in greater detail.

Arbitrage

This is the only type of trading that makes use of price differentials in order to offer you an unrisky profit. Any trading strategy comes with a certain amount of risk, however when it is used correctly Arbitrage trading can come near in terms of being completely risk free.

Arbitrage trading is when the security being traded is not in line with the fair value assigned to it. Usually, it involves the purchase of the security and then trade it off with the same security in order to reap the advantages of market inefficiencies.

If arbitrage is properly structured it is necessary for the trade to be neutral, meaning that it removes risk. The risk here is a sudden move in the market which could cause the trade to be unstable.

The most significant risk associated with investing in arbitrage is the fact that market's behavior isn't always predictable It is also possible that the trades take a different direction, rather than moving in a direct relation. A good instance is when a major investor pushes the stock significantly lower through the sale of all stake they own in the company. The price will decrease for a short period of time.

Merger Arbitrage

This type of trading can be riskier for the investor. It involves buying shares of a company following the imminent buyout and taking advantage of the difference between the purchase price and the price of buyout. This is because the company being purchased typically trades at a discount in comparison to the price at which the buyout is made.

Example

Imagine that a corporation X announces a buyout offer to Company Y at $20 per share. Company The price of shares may go initially at $18.90. In this case shareholders of the company X may not want to wait many months until the deal is completed in order to earn an additional $1.10 in the event of a they earn. They could decide to trade the shares they own and earn an income right now.

If you are an arbitrage trader you consider this $1.10 gain as goldmine, particularly in the case of a low risk involved in the transaction. There is a chance of the merger being cancelled. It is possible to earn a substantial profit by purchasing shares for $18.90 and then waiting for the deal's closing and then sell the shares for a profit.

Financial Arbitrage

It is the term used to describe the trading of foreign exchange. It is the practice of going short and long at the same time when exchanging two kinds of currencies. If you look up the exchange rates of currencies of the different exchanges, it becomes apparent that they are different. This means that you may purchase the currency at one exchange and then sell it at another exchange in order to make profits.

Example

Broker A provides the USD/EUR pair for 5/3 dollars per euro. A different broker B also offers the pair for 5/4 dollars for each euro. then you could convert 10 euros into USD using the broker that you used previously and then change to convert the USD in EUR using broker B. This results in a the possibility of earning.

Statistics Arbitrage (StatArb)

The details of this kind of arbitrage goes beyond the scope of this book, but you have to be aware of the fact that it's very like pairs trading, but at a higher cost.

People who invest using this kind of arbitrage can find hundreds of stocks that are predicted to move similarly in accordance with statistical reference points, but in different directions. In order to make statistical calculations trading, traders use complex software. They profit from price changes by trading stocks that are in both long and short-term positions, but this is dependent on the type of commodity.

Example

If a trader believes the Facebook stocks are overvalued or Amazon shares are priced at a lower value, they can take a long position on Facebook as well as a short one on Amazon this is known in pairs trading.

Dividend Arbitrage

This involves the purchase of a certain amount of stock and put options of the same amount. It is best to do this prior to the dividend expires date. If you receive dividends, you can use your put option.

But, you must employ complex mathematical formulas as well as a lot of experience to do this happen.

Example

Imagine that the stock AB is being traded at $100 per share, and will pay dividends of $3 per share in the span of a week. It is possible to buy shares and receive the dividends within just a week.

Retail arbitrage

In the same way that you employ arbitrage in financial markets you can also do the same using your typical supermarket for regular retail products. For example, a glance at eBay will show you a variety of goods that are available for a cheap cost in China however they're priced higher on a different site.

Example

Purchase an item at Wal-Mart and then sell it through Amazon or eBay for the profit.

Convertible Arbitrage

It is a method of purchasing convertible securities and selling the stock that was the source of the security.

Example

Goodyear has decided to sell its tires in order to clear its stock at a price of $60. The tires are priced at $90 in other markets. It is possible to purchase the tires and then reap the gains that go along with it.

Negative Arbitrage

Most often this chance is missed due to the fact that the rate of interest the borrower pays on the loan is greater than the rate for the fund being put to work.

Example

Let's say that a city council decides to construct a road and issue bonds worth $100,000,000 in municipal bonds of 6% to fund the construction cost. Because of the change in interest rates the council earns only 3% on the accounts, while paying bondholders 6%. They lose 33% due in negative arbitage.

The opportunities for arbitrage usually arise in many different situations:

* Stocks that have different share classes.

* Stocks listed in multiple exchanges. For example, we may have a share that is trading mostly in Australia but listed in Canada too.

* Stocks that are tied with specific markets for the future.

In order for the event to occur, it must be two comparable securities, but they have different prices. It is only a circumstance that can yield you profits due to the differences in prices across different markets.

Traders who use this method of trading are referred to as arbitrageurs. The theory is based on the concept of market efficiency which states that in order for the market to function efficiently, there cannot be any arbitrage opportunities . All the equivalent securities should be convergent to the same value. The convergence of prices is the most accurate indicator of the market's efficiency.

A perfect example of arbitrage trading

In the year Warren Buffet was six years old, he figured out that he could buy the coca cola 6-pack at 25 cents . He could then sell a bottle of the pack for 5 cents, making a profit of 5 cents per pack. He realized that he could make money by the variation in cost of the pack as compared to what the consumers could purchase each bottle for.

Conditions that are required for arbitration to occur

Arbitrage can only take place if these conditions are met:

* The presence of an asset price imbalance. This could take place in a variety of types, like the same asset being traded on different markets, or assets with the same cash flow being traded at different prices , and when an asset has a future price that is known is traded at a cost lower than the future cash value.

The simultaneous trading. In this case, the buying and selling of similar assets has to be done simultaneously in order that it is able to capture price variations. If the trades aren't executed simultaneously, the trade is at risk.

Arbitrage in Retail

Although retail traders can benefit from the financial instruments offered at different brokerages with different rates, it's a challenge to attain. The intense market competition ensures that the prices will remain identical, with a few exceptions. This means that a lot of brokers will not earn a significant amount of money from trades, which in way limits trades. If you take transaction cost into consideration it is apparent that the opportunities are virtually nonexistent.

Another Illustration

Let's suppose that a company that is a stock trades at $20 in the London Stock Exchange, and traders discover that the stock is traded at $20.80 in the New York Stock Exchange, then the trader is able to purchase the stock from the LSE and then sell it for profit on NYSE which will earn $0.80 for each stock.

But, you must be aware that you may not be the only one who recognizes this opportunity and many traders are looking for the same thing. This is why you should make use of Algorithmic trading programs that recognize the opportunity and take the opportunity before others take advantage of it.

Be aware that once the demand for the stock increases that the cheaper stock will appreciate within the LSE and the increasing demand of the NYSE will push the higher priced stock lower.

Currencies are among the most well-known securities used to trade arbitrage. In contrast to asset trading, currency do not have to be traded through central exchanges but instead can be traded through over-the-counter markets all over the world.

Benefits of arbitrage trading

The most significant benefit in arbitrage trades is the fact that they reduces the risk. If you do the proper study and finding markets that are able to sell the stock for a higher price, you can be sure of profiting by trading.

The increasing popularity of arbitrage trading allows for the prices of the securities on the market to settle. It keeps the price of the securities on the market at a steady level which means that it can end the price fluctuations across various markets.

* By using this strategy for trading the financial markets become more efficient due to the confidence of investors confidence in their investment.

The disadvantages of trading arbitrage

Most traders do not consider the issue of transaction costs and focus only on the cost aspect for the securities. Transactions that include taxes or other hidden costs could provide a false estimate of profits and lead to losses instead of profit.

It is possible that you won't have the chance to take advantage of as numerous arbitrage opportunities like you'd like. In addition, if opportunities arise they require the most recent trading software in order to quickly identify opportunities and earn a profit. The knowledge required to profit from these opportunities isn't available for many.

* You require a substantial capital investment to make the most of arbitrage. Most arbitrage opportunities yield profits in cents, so you'll need additional funds in order to reap the rewards.

Momentum Trading

Momentum trading, like the name suggests seeks to profit of the market trends in securities - both upward as well as downward movements in price.

Investors who employ this method think that trends will go on in this direction over a particular time due to the momentum created behind the security. Let's take a examine the various types of momentum that you have to be aware of in order to profit from this kind of trading.

Price Momentum

One of the most effective strategies to apply to this kind of trading is price momentum. If you intend to employ this model as a basis for making your decisions, you will need examine the stocks that have been moving upwards every day every week, week after week, or perhaps for a period of time. In order to do this you must be armed with evidence to show that markets which are at their highest level will remain at the top for a longer period of time.

However, this form of strategy is much more unstable in comparison to the other types of strategies. This kind of trading makes use of the high volatility that the markets have. In other words, if you fail to make sure to time your sells and buys correctly it could result in you ending in losses. It is important to employ methods of risk management (such like stop-loss) to reduce the risk of losing money.

It is also essential to have the proper settings on the trading platform, so that you are able to identify stocks that trade at a premium for a long time.

Example

In the middle of 2008 the energy and oil sector saw a steady rise in the cost of its securities. It was then among the top sectors that utilized the measures that are based on 12-week and 24-week forecasts. Even though the market was struggling however, it was profitable for the majority of traders due to the massive gains.

As an investor, you have be aware of patterns early. It is possible that you consider including a short-term price change to your calculations like two weeks or a four-week price measurement.

In order to be a successful momentum trader, it is essential to be able to recognize the most profitable sectors quickly and with precision. You can accomplish this by with the many manual screeners available.

How do you determine the most profitable sectors to use for Momentum Trading

Select the stocks you would like to trade.

* Find the percentage of stocks trading close to their annual highests.

Sort the stocks based on their performance, ranging from low to high.

* Create an entry strategy. Choose whether you'd like to join the market when the price is showing its best performance or wait in the event of weakness in the stock.

• Have an exit strategy. Be aware of when you can enter the trade and when you'd like to be in the trade.

Tools to use to Advanced Momentum Trading

There are a range of tools for technical analysis to make profit using the strategy of momentum trading. These options include chart reader, moving averages oscillators and relative strength. These tools are available on all different trading systems you'll be joining. But, it is important to find and select the top tools that compliment each other and provide the most effective outcomes.

The general rule is that the performance of any stock will be stronger at the beginning of the trend. It is also it is weakest in the time that the market is getting close to reverse. It is possible to think of a ball which accelerates rapidly when it leaves your hands and then slows at the time of its peak, before returning back to its original position.

To ride the waves of any momentum it is essential to tweak the indicators of technical analysis that indicate an investment worthwhile to invest in. Be aware of when to stop typically, as evident by the slowing of momentum.

Let's look at the analytical tools used in technical analysis of the area of momentum trading.

The main source of information for the majority of investors begins with the analysis of technical aspects. It is about determining how solid each asset is relative to its price. Any trader should be aware of the most important indicators is an essential aspect of the strategy for trading.

1. Trend lines

This tool is perfect for monitoring price changes. The trend line connects two points that are consecutive on the price chart. If the line is inclined upwards, the signal indicates a favorable direction, an ideal signal for the investor to invest in shares. If the line slopes downwards, then the trend is negative, and trading short would be the most effective place to change.

2. Moving Average

The moving average can help traders identify a dominant trend, while removing non-essential signals that result from tiny price movements. If the price is stable or rises above the average, it is an upward trend. A negative trend is usually observed when the price is lower than its moving average.

3. Stochastic Oscillator

If you want to evaluate the closing price of an asset's value and its price over time, this is the best indicator. When the closing price is close to the top, it is trending upwards and if the price at which it closes is lower, the trend is negative.

The indicators vary from 0 to 100. The numbers between 51 and 100 are indicative of positive trends, while numbers that are below 50 suggest negative trends.

4. Average Directional Index

It is also known as ADX This indicator of momentum is most well-known since it is thought to be less likely to generate an untrue signal as other indicators like the Stochastic Oscillator. This indicator is perfect for determining whether there is an ongoing trend and how strong it is.

The index's values vary all the way from zero up to. If the index is below 25, it indicates an unfocused variation, meaning that the market is not showing a clear direction. Anything that is above 25 indicates that there is an underlying trend. Higher readings indicate a more significant trend. A 50-point value in the index will be more powerful than a reading of 40 for the exact index.

Things You Must Focus on Momentum Trading

Since momentum trading is based on the use of the short-term price movement of the commodity, you need be sure to focus on some aspects that determine the direction you make. Here are some of the things you should look for:

a. The Volume of stock

This is the amount of shares exchanged on the markets. Because the goal of moving stocks is to move into and out of a trade on one day it is essential that there are plenty of traders available for the commodity on the market. It is essential to concentrate on stocks that have a high volume, which can allow you to enter an investment and exit more quickly. Also, stocks with a large trade volumes have greater liquidity, which means they is able to be traded rapidly.

b. The Time Frame

We will examine the time period during which stocks move. Typically, momentum trading demands quick moves, rather than longer-term movements. There is no concern about what happens one month or a year from now. This is that momentum traders don't take the time to examine the reputation of the company as companies that are not good can see remarkable price swings within a very short period of time and a great business could be overlooked for years.

C. Variatility as well as Range

If you're a trader focused on moving markets, there's something that can make you feel more excited than an investment that's volatile in the market. It is important to ensure that you are able to make significant movements in the market. A stock that has been stuck in the exact same spot for many hours can provide you with a small trading chance.

D. Analysis of technical aspects

Although investors tend to place much emphasis on the condition of the company they are investing in however, momentum traders in contrast are focused on the particular stock. The only thing you have to focus on is price action as in the realm of momentum trading it is the stock that is the sole product.

E. Catalysts

These triggers cause the stock fall or to break out. You should focus than the consequences that triggers the stock, but rather the reaction that the market experiences in response to triggers. If, for instance, there's a security concern within the country, and the prices of several companies that are related to it rise. This might not be logical, but it certainly created numerous trading opportunities. Knowing how the catalyst influences price is most effective method to assess the price for the share.

F. The Risk is versus. Reward

Many consider trading as a type of gambling. If you follow the rules you'll reap the same advantages. What makes them different is the fact that the trader does an extensive risk analysis to determine the most effective way to proceed.

In every activity there is a either risk or rewarding. This being said it is imperative to discover ways to reduce the risk and increase the benefits. When we trade momentum We look for products with an acceptable risk-to-reward ratio.

If, for instance, you decide to trade without the proper planning there is the chance of making an income that is considered to be gamble. But if you look at the patterns and conduct a thorough analysis, you can discover favorable settings that will give you the lowest risk.

g. The Strength of the Sector

Certain industries run at different times. Certain industries are in operation as new regulations are enacted and others are active when there are news stories regarding the industry. It is important to be aware of these trends as they can assist in understanding the diverse changes in the sector. This also provides you with an opportunity to locate trading opportunities within the sector.

H. Stock Trends

It is essential to concentrate on the trend of particular stocks. If you notice an uptrend throughout the day it is important to take the correct decision to ensure that you do not increase the risk.

i. The strength of the market

You must be attentive to the strength and weakness of the market to know the underlying dynamics of these markets. It is possible to do this by examining the different indexes of major firms like NASDAQ.

j. Trading Setups

Many traders have been observed to overlook this fact in their trading. Before you take a position in an investment, you have to be able to provide a reason. It is important to understand the reasons behind why you're buying that stock at the price you are currently paying. The reason you are entering it shouldn't be based on the belief that the price will rise afterward, since that doesn't sound like a good justification. You must have a reason that is connected to the risk:reward ratio or the chance of the price breaking out.

Risks of Momentum Trading Risks of Momentum Trading

* There is no absolute assurance that the demands of purchasing will push the cost of the commodity up.

* If a large number of investors already have large positions on the stocks It is possible that the existing positions will outweigh new traders who enter this market eventually pushing the prices to fall and result in losses.

* There is no assurance it will last. It is because something may not be happening since it took place yesterday or even the week prior to.

If you're not familiar with how to read the signals, you could be unable to recognize the beginning of an trend. That means you'll miss out on early profit too.

Trend following

Trend following is a method to identify patterns and gain profit from the trends. There are several methods to do this, but keep in mind that no one indicator will provide you with the returns you're entitled to, as trading is a mix of different factors like managing risk, trading psychology and more.

The fundamental principle behind trend following is to follow the trend that is in place in the present - purchase when prices are in an upward trend and sell when it is in a downward direction. It is not your goal to predict or forecast the future; all you need to do is be aware of different markets and look for trends that are emerging.

What is the reason Trend Following works? The reason is straightforward - trading is governed by emotion - fear and greed. This trading strategy has proven successful over the last 200 years because of a variety of factors.

Strategies for Successfully Methods to Successfully Follow Trends

The foundation of the Trend Following technique are five fundamental principles that will ensure you achieve the success you require.

1. Buy High and sell Low

You must find securities you can purchase at a lower cost and then sell them at an increased price in order to earn an income. The difference in price is what makes the profit. Prices for commodities at different exchanges can vary which is why this should be the primary thing you look at. For example, when trading stocks, try to buy them at a bargain price , and sell them at a price that is sufficiently high to offer you a return.

2. Be sure to know your Costs

You'll want to stay on the right path always. It's always good to know that you bought the correct price at the right time and made the correct purchase.

However, there's one drawback - when you begin to make predictions, it can impair your judgment and lose the objectiveness that you set out to attain. This can result in a the inability to accept losses because of the desire to always be correct and averaging losses as it is impossible to go further right now, and retribution trading because you're trying to recover the money you lost.

What you must do as a trend-follower, is to keep an eye on the price and react in accordance with the price. If you are aware you are seeing the prices getting more and more lower it is likely that an uptrend is on the horizon, and you should be looking to invest in. If you observe the price making lower lows, you can bet that it's on the downward side and you must be trying to short it.

3. Learn to manage risks

If you've got a system which only offers the minimum amount of profit, regardless of how long you trade, you should know exactly the amount you should put in to ensure that you earn a profit. It is essential that you develop an effective strategy that includes risk management to are able to recover any losses you face. To achieve this, you have to be aware of the percentage loss you suffer in the capital and the proportion of profit you must earn in order to make up the loss.

If, for instance, your losses are 50 percent or more of your capital, it's recommended to make a return of 100 percent of your capital, particularly if there is a win-win rate that is less then 50 percent.

4. Markets to Trade in All Markets to increase the odds

If you decide to use Trends, you're trying to earn more profit on the upward and downward trend. If you are a trend follower you are able to trade everything from currencies, metals bonds, energy, agricultural and indexes.

Trend Following Indicators

To benefit from the benefits trend-following has to offer it is essential to be on the lookout in the market for new trends. The trends that are emerging can be seen by using indicators of trend. But, no one indicator will provide you with the ideal method to purchase or sell the stock. But, there are a few indicators that are frequently used to give an accurate perspective and help you to make informed decisions.

1. Moving Averages

It is an extremely popular indicator that is used to make a decision which isn't based solely on the fluctuation of prices. The indicator utilizes the historical data which can be used to analyze the changes in prices over a certain time. The data also shows the direction in which the trend will follow.

With the help of the moving averages method, you are able to decide whether you should choose a short or long position on any commodity. If the price of the stock is showing declining trends, you are able to decide to sell any stock you own. In contrast, if the stock exhibits progress, you are able to purchase more stocks due to the belief that the stock will move higher.

Before you can plot your moving average you have to determine the time period, before you decide on the stock to examine.

2. Bollinger Bands

The indicators which are displayed along a line display the fluctuations in price of a specific stock. They include three lines, the higher middle, lower, and upper Bollinger band. The lower and upper Bollinger bands represent 2 standard deviations to the average. They can be used to assess the level of volatility of various prices.

After you have plotted the bands The following step will be to apply them to gauge the volatility of the market. If the market becomes increasingly volatile, then the gap between the two indicators grows while the opposite is true for situations with low volatility. If the volatility is excessive it is time to stop trading.

3. Moving Average Convergence Divergence

Abbreviated ad MACD is a comparative analysis which analyzes two moving averages of different data sets. Utilizing the resultant bandwidth of the series, you are able to analyze the price fluctuations of two time-based datasets.

The comparison of the moving averages of the data sets is by analyzing the convergence of data, dramatic rise and divergence.

4. On Balance Volume

This is a signpost that examines the flow of the volume in order to establish the direction the trend is heading. The quantity and the increase in price are generally directly proportional. If the OBV increases, it is a strong indication that the price is also rising and reverse is also true.

5. Relative Strength Index

The abbreviation is simply RSI The calculation of this indicator using the formula below:

RSI = 100-100/ (1+RS)

RS in this sense refers to the average of gains from up and down periods within a particular time period. This indicator displays the rate and changes in price. It gives an understanding of the way security is performing on the stock market. It provides you with a number between

0 to 100, based on the strength of the security on the market.

Different types of trend followers

Two kinds of traders utilize this method to earn money:

Systematic Trend Followers

They use quantitative indicators to help you get into and out of trades. Common indicators employed include MACt or moving averages. A systematic trader may purchase when the market is beyond the daily 50 moving averages, based on the belief that it's in an upward trend in the event that it goes over the 50-point mark. If the market drops below the 50-point threshold the expert who follows the trend chooses to sell the security since they are trapped in a market in downtrend.

Disretionary Trend Followers

These traders employ the pattern of breakdown and breakout to decide on their strategy. If the market breaks out of a pattern of resistance The trader purchases and then decides to sell when they believe that the market has retreated from an established pattern.

The advantages of following trends

You'll Be able to Keep Track of All Movements

If you follow this method it is possible to profit from big and small moves while making money by leveraging the strategy. If the market fluctuates from up to down it will provide you with the signal to purchase. If the market is moving in a significant way it is possible to earn massive profits from your investment.

Huge Profit Margins

The potential profit for this strategy, particularly when you make use of the long-term trends, is greater. The benefit is that even if the likelihood of profit is lower than 50 however, you can still gain from your investment. This is only feasible when you boost the amount of the winning trade contrasted to the number of losses. If done correctly, one trade could be all you require for generating profits that last all year.

Reduce the cost of your purchase

Another benefit to this approach is that you will reduce costs over the course of a few months and also through more trades. The long-term can lower the cost of transactions as well.

Capacity to reduce losses

If you make use of long-term trends you can make use of the proof idea of reducing expenses while increasing your profit. This is achievable if you stay with the trend for a period of months or even years.

The drawbacks of following trends

As there are benefits for using this strategy for trading but we also face the disadvantages of the strategy.

More losers than winners

If you are you employ the trading technique you will experience more loss trades than you do successful ones. The main reason for this is that markets are only trending 20% all the time.

Furthermore, losses can occur when you try to identify the beginning of a lucrative trend, which is a difficult method. In addition, as the market is volatile all the time and timing the conclusion of this cycle may cause false signals prior to you take advantage of opportunities.

Boredom

As the market changes just about 20% often, this could result in boredom trading is the primary goal is trade! As an investor, you want to participate in trading and earn money. A life of solitary sitting with a little chance of success isn't enjoyable.

This is especially true for traders who work at the computer screen for hours at a time. The hours could go on without a proper signal making it difficult for traders to make a decision at all.

The computer screen for hours on end can result in distractions. You might discover yourself reading emails or playing video games while you look again on your computer, you realize that you've have missed a fantastic trade.

Trade driven by factors

This is a system for trading which is backed by research conducted by top academics and market players. It is based on the experience of professional investors who have had to endure. It is easy to use but it provides an approach that minimizes the risk of investing and provides you the highest return on your investment.

Similar to other studies in the field, the market for finance has been subjected to rigorous tests with lots of information. The results have been compared to strict peer review processes, and have found the same results regardless of the other researchers who have gone through the tests.

These data and statistics can be be established beyond doubt and constitute the primary driver for investors to in order to earn profits.

There are two kinds of factors used to make choices: macroeconomic and style factors. Macroeconomic factors focus on broad risks that are inherent in diverse asset clauses whereas the style factors concentrate on describing the risks which are inherent to the various assets.

Components of Factors Investment

Different elements of factor investing comprise:

Value

This is a way to determine the amount of returns you can expect from stocks with very low prices relative to their initial value. This is typically tracked using dividends, price to earnings ratio, price to value or free cash flow.

Size

Size refers to the market value that the company has. An examination of historical data will show that small-cap stocks yield more profits in comparison to portfolios with large-cap stocks.

Quality

The hallmark of quality is steady earnings and low debt levels, solid corporate governance, and consistent growth in assets. Investors can spot high-quality companies using common indicators like debt to equity and return to equity and earnings fluctuation.

Momentum

It is well-known that stocks that previously exceeded expectations usually have strong returns in the future. It is important to monitor the momentum in the 3 to 12 months.

Volatility

When you trade in the market, it is important to know that stocks with low volatility, yield better returns than assets with higher volatility.

Strategies to create the perfect factor-based strategy are:

• Making up an idea for trading or a strategy for investing that you are planning to apply.

* Determining various aspects to be used as the basis for making the right choice.

* Acquiring the pertinent information.

150

* Analyzing all the aspects and forming the best strategy.

* Backtesting and evaluating the strategy.

The strategy is implemented.

Mean Reversion

Mean reversion is based with the assumption that there exists an underpinning steady trend in the value of a security, and that price fluctuations will occur randomly in line with the trend. It also assumes that prices that diverge from the trend, will be inclined to reverse before returning back to the original trend.

If the value is high, we anticipate that the price will fall lower, and when it's unusually low the price will return up.

The most important question is what is the trend's initial value? This is the core of the method we will discuss.

To determine the trend that is underlying to determine the underlying trend, we use an average of long-term movement, like 90 days. We then apply that as stable trend. If the value drops below the original value then we anticipate the value to rise. If prices are too high, then we anticipate it to rise which is the signal to invest.

In the same way, if the price rises and we believe that it will drop toward the value that is in the beginning this is a great signal to sell.

In order to make a sale that is successful it is essential to ensure that you are aware of your indicators. Here are some indicators you can utilize to determine when it is right to sale or purchase.

* Relative Strength Indicator (RSI)

* Bollinger bands.

* ConnorRSI.

* Stretching Average.

*The number of days that are down.

* Change in rate.

When deciding on the strategy, it is important to set goals. There are a variety of metrics to determine the objectives however the most crucial measure is called the COMPounded Annual Return.

The Mean Reversion Strategy

In order to apply the strategy of mean reversion successfully it is necessary to choose the currency pair you want to use. It and then calculate the average cost. You must look at every trading range you can find which includes short-term and long-term.

If you use mean reversion, you remove all the risk out of trading. When you are a beginner in trading it is common to guess the activities you engage in during the beginning of trading. This typically results in losses. These losses can impact the confidence of the trader's ability to trade.

If a currency pair's price is significantly lower than the average, it is a perfect signal to purchase. This signals that the price is likely to increase. If, however, it is higher than the average , it is likely to fall back to the mean, signalling that it is moment to sell.

When should you use Mean Reversion?

Mean reversion is a good option for trades with a short duration that are evident in extremely unstable conditions. Avoid using mean reversion in long-term trading because you'll lose the money. The method is suitable for trades that are short-term and won't last longer than a few minutes or even hours.

When you're using the strategy of mean reversion, avoid charts with the highest or lowest levels. Long dips like this are not common and easily are noticeable. The existence of long dips suggests that the price won't reverse anytime soon.

The most successful trader for this kind of strategy is one who will be willing to take large risks to earn greater reward. If you want to enjoy the advantages this strategy can offer you must turn off your emotional inclinations and make your choice based on data.

The advantages of Mean Reversion

These strategies for Mean Reversion have extremely short periods of between three and seven days. This is why they are effective in times of high volatility.

Demerits

When the volatility is low, transactions are in cash, which can be very frustrating. The best way to trade is without stops. This means that you must be patient till the value to recover.

It can be difficult to make a trade since the charts are usually cluttered.

Scaling

The scalping strategy is among the most well-known strategies that is ideal for both short-term retail and traders in the institutional market. Instead of seeking enormous gains from one trade it is a way to improve the win-to-loss ratio by spreading them out across multiple trades. The process involves tiny trades that yield tiny profits, which will multiply into huge profits over time.

This strategy for trading is perfect for traders who have to make transactions that are short-term but have access to huge capital expenditure. For success you must have the discipline to be a top performer and discipline, particularly when you're not making use of any automated trading platform for buying and selling securities.

The benefits of Scalping

Limited Risks

These strategies are intended to minimize risk effectively. Single trades carry a significant risk. Therefore, it is advisable to spread risk over several smaller trades, so that you don't lose your money on one trade.

Do not have to wait around for directions

This strategy doesn't need the movement of a particular stock toward a certain direction in order in order to gain. This means that you can gain from moves to either side , either up or down.

Simple Automation

They are simple to incorporate into a trading system that you prefer. The primary reason for this is that the method is based on precise technical information that is simple to calculate.

The drawbacks of the Scalping Strategy

Requires a Greater Minimum

This method demands you to have more money in your account to ensure that you can adhere to trading regulations and make the profits you need to meet your objectives.

More expensive costs

Because you're running more than one trade at a time, you will be liable for more costs in the future.

Need to Control

This strategy needs the use of a lot of leverage to generate enough profits. It is therefore essential to maintain a high degree of control in order to can avoid losing money.

The implementation of Scalping Strategy

If you are deciding to apply scalping strategies it is important to use a couple of tried and tried strategies:

* Decide on the indicators you'll employ and then define the way you'll use them.

You should run a test backwards so that you can see how the strategy could have performed if it was used before.

* Paper trade is the strategy you've selected by using broker quotes.

Once you have decided on the strategy, proceed and make the necessary changes to the strategy so that you can reduce the risk at stake.

After the strategy has been put in place The next step is to begin using the strategy, while monitoring the outcomes. Keep yourself up to date with any developments that may impact the market.

Sentiment Analysis

Sentiment analysis is a sure method to determine the mindset of traders and is regarded as a great method for many. This is because every trader has their own view on how things work on the marketplace. Based on the opinion of the market, traders decide what direction to trade in either to purchase or sell.

Every trader has his own thoughts and opinions. These are expressed in the position they choose to take when they trade. This creates market's sentiment, regardless of the details available.

The problem is that, as retail trader, regardless of however strongly you are about every trade, you can't influence the market to your favour. For example, if you believe that the value of the dollar will appreciate or that the value of a share will soon double, and everybody else doesn't share the same opinion there's nothing you can do to do.

As traders, it's your responsibility to conduct the analysis of sentiment. It is your responsibility to figure out what the market's mood is and whether it's bullish or bearish. Then you need to integrate this knowledge in your strategy for trading.

It is possible to choose to ignore the market's sentiments However, keep in mind that it's your decision and you may be losing. Keep in mind that what is important isn't the way you feel or think, it's what is a consensus among the market. This is what determines the price for the investment.

The sentiment in the market could be negative, positive, or neutral. The base is macroeconomic news, world events as well as technical analysis fundamental analysis, as well as economic reports that are not related to the economy.

There are two kinds of feelings:

Bullish Sentiment

The market is bullish when the mood towards the marketplace is favorable. When a market is bullish it is when prices are predicted to increase.

Bearish sentiment

The mood is bullish in the event that it's negative. In an economic downturn, this occurs when prices begin falling.

However it is possible that the sentiment trading may also be mean reverting , or contrary, meaning that it is contrary to market's general sentiment. The theory operates by assuming that if there is a huge crowd in relation to a specific trade then it can lead to an exploitation, and the trade that results is then followed by a drop or rise in price because of corrections, and reverse.

Sentiment Indicators

Sentiment indicators are signals which tell you where public opinion of the market is. The indicators could be qualitative like opinions polls. Numerous firms provide the information that you require from trading and marketing professionals. They conduct surveys, polls and then release these.

The surveys that companies conduct are conducted regularly and reports are published or sold as a set. They are organized with graphs and visuals to ensure you are aware of every sentiment.

In addition, you could make use of quantitative market data including trading volume, security price as well as open interest. A few of these indicators are:

* Arms Index

* Ratio of Put/Call

* VIX

* Cash position of mutual funds

* Margin debt

* Short interest rate

Machine Learning-Based Trading

In this type of Algorithmic trading, Artificial Intelligence takes center in making predictions about the range of price movements. Typically, it is able to provide an immediate duration. The benefit of using this approach is that humans design an initial trading platform while the AI develops the trading algorithm and enhances it in time.

The majority of models that were previously used were static, meaning that they don't alter with the changes on the market. Models based on ML can analyse a large amount of data at high speeds , and then enhance the system based on the results.

The models that are used in trading are:

Bayesian Networks

It is a type of machine learning, which can be used to forecast the developments in the market using a variety of machines. The network makes use of a type of computation that is run across hundreds of machines and computers to make the correct calculation.

161

The AI will create random stock traders , and then proceed to test their historical performance. Then, it seeks out the most effective methods and then creates a list of traders. The system then repeats this procedure several times, and finally ends with a trading system which can operate entirely by itself.

Smart Beta Trading

Beta refers to the degree of volatility in an investment or security when compared to the broader market. In a market, such as that of the market for stocks, the individual securities are classified in relation to the extent they differ in relation to the beta.

The first smart beta exchange traded fund hit the marketplace in the year 2003 and, after that the variety of funds that are available rapidly. The primary reason is that investors are seeking alternative options for free that are not too expensive cost to offer the option of actively managing funds.

This method gives the possibility of running an investment that is passive that are focused on cutting costs and generating a profit.

The pattern of trading is different from traditional indices which weight down the constituents based on the size of the market. A more intelligent beta index may be named after smaller businesses that are more likely to outperform later. The primary stocks that profit by this method are those that have ones with value-based earnings, those which are gaining momentum, and those that are less volatile in the market.

The reaction of traders was overwhelming, and there's been a flurry of products in the marketplace that means that more and increasing investors have been investing into indexes.

Smart beta indices are different in comparison to traditional strategies for trading in of applying a set of objective guidelines to each index of the business. They are then ranked on their scores on the various elements.

Chapter 11: Back Testing

A majority of the research related to algorithm trading is an empirical study. This is a reference to past experiences and observations of the market. This contrasts with the theoretical research which is more based on assumptions or logic or mathematical structures.

Backtesting is the process of testing the trading strategy you're considering by replicating it with historical data in order to assess whether the strategy works today. The process of conducting tests is an essential component of determining the best trading strategy and also in the creation of the ideal trading strategy for your needs.

Backtesting is based on the notion that what worked in the past is likely to be successful in the near future. In the reverse, it is also true If a system has failed before, it is likely to not work in the present.

Chart 3: place for backtesting during trading Algorithmic development

By comparing statistics from a historical standpoint, you can decide whether a method you're contemplating is effective when you apply it. If it's not working then you'll be able to discover weaknesses in the strategy, after which you can modify it to fit your requirements.

Keep in mind that backtesting analyses is time-consuming, particularly in the case of real results. Before you are able to arrive at the best results, you'll need to collect a lot of information from reliable sources.

Backtesting is essential because it lets us examine a variety of concepts or models quickly and easily, and thus provide immediate feedback about how different systems performed over time.

The reasons behind backtesting an Algorithmic Strategy

Filtration

Filtration is the process of creating a pipeline for strategy to filter any strategy that does not meet the set-down criteria. Backtesting gives traders an effective filtering mechanism since we are able to remove any strategies that don't satisfy specific performance requirements.

Modeling

Backtesting lets traders test the new model in a particular market, like the routing of orders, transaction costs as well as liquidity, latency and many other.

Optimization

It's a known fact that strategies optimization has several biases but backtesting allows traders to improve the performance of a strategy via modification of the number or the values of various parameters related to the strategy.

Verification

If you sort the methods, you will get the ones you believe will work the best. However, some strategies aren't implemented, and it is essential the use of a plan to get rid of these. Testing backwards can ensure that the plan has been applied in line with established criteria.

Before proceeding further, we must consider the benefits you will get from performing backtesting.

The Benefits of Backtesting

Ability to test before deployment

Backtesting is a method of testing the technical aspects of a strategy that is to be employed in trading. With this technique you can evaluate the effectiveness of a given strategy and see if similar results were obtained before.

If you've achieved the outcomes you're seeking, you can look at the current numbers to determine whether the strategy has an accurate value or not.

Increases confidence

The process of backtesting your trading strategies can helps build confidence in traders regarding a planned strategy prior to the time you implement it into the current market. It's based on the notion that, if the method been successful before it will work in the future.

Improves the value of a proposition

Backtesting that is properly executed can determine if an idea is able to maintain its advantage or is not in what circumstances it might be manifested. By adjusting the various parameters, you are able to check how strong the concept is. The trader can pinpoint the market conditions in which the edge can be traded or even significant.

It helps you understand the Win-Rate Percentage

Backtesting can reveal the most likely win-loss ratio and informs you the winning and percentages of losing

Be aware of the expected results prior to taking action

Understanding the different issues surrounding the Algorithmic aids you in determining under what circumstances the concept is a tradeable idea.

Backtesting is not without its limitations.

One of the biggest drawbacks to backtesting is it may make you believe that you are in over your head because of the way the system has performed previously. There's always a risk in believing that a system will perform in the way you want it to, but it fails. Keep in mind that the market is a complicated system that cannot give traders identical results repeatedly. Even if you conduct the perfect backtest , with the ability to predict in the future, you'll likely to see a gap from the real results to backtest results once you are live.

Important Factors to Consider prior to testing backtests

Before you decide to begin the backtesting process You must consider the various aspects.

1. Past Performances Do Not Mean Future Prosperity

Backtesting relies on the most recent data to determine what is likely to occur in the near future. But, it is important be aware that the results that were achieved in the past do not necessarily ensure success in the future either. Markets can be volatile and could change at any moment, which can impact the effectiveness of results that were derived by backtesting.

2. The Results aren't 100% accurate

For any kind of market, such as for instance in the Forex market there are a myriad of factors that influence the way that trades are conducted. In particular, usage of spreads that differ by traders can affect outcomes. Also, volatility can affect the results since you're employing two strategies that are similar with different settings. The best part is that when using the Algorithmic approach to trading, you are left with fewer mistakes than performing everything manually.

3. Live trades are different

The process of trading live in the current market is not the same as working with data from the past. There is a high chance of trading too slow or making numerous mistakes to keep up with the current market conditions.

4. Variable Results

They can arise when you choose to trade large quantities. This is due to the fact that the process of trading large can produce diverse results each time. In addition, large-scale orders can be prone to the bizarre ability to alter the value of a security in any direction.

Furthermore, backtesting comes with many biases. We will take a look at some aspects of those biases within the following section.

Backtesting methods

There are two kinds of backtesting strategies you can test both manual and automated backtesting. Automated backtesting is based with a program created by the user, while the trades are put in place based on a set of factors. In contrast manual backtesting needs the user to analyze charts and conditions in detail and then make trades based on the rules you create.

If you know programming languages, you can automate backtesting. However, you must keep in mind the current market conditions and adapt your code and strategy to meet the current market circumstances. If you don't, it can result in incorrect results due to the changes in market conditions.

The most important things to consider When deciding on the best Backtesting Methodology

Before you can come up with the correct backtesting method, you must ensure you think about the following aspects:

* Choose the Right Market Segment

It is essential to select the correct market segment so that you can come up with the best backtesting method. It is important to take into consideration a variety of factors , which include the risks that you're willing accept as well as the risk that is inherent in the market. Also, you must consider the potential profit you're hoping to earn and also the period you'll be investing into the markets.

Consider the time frame you intend to invest for whether it is short term or long-term so you know the type of asset which are suitable for your method of trading.

* Look at the Data

The prices that are prevalent on the market are subject to a variety of factors and continue fluctuating based on the present situation. These include the policies of monetary policy, annual corporate statements, the rate of inflation and much more.

The primary thing you must consider is the fact that markets do not behave in the same manner which is why you must examine the strategies in order that you can understand how they will work under various conditions.

* Find the Right Platform for Coding

There are many platforms can be used to carry out backtesting of the data. We will look into these platforms in the coming weeks but in short it is important to understand how well the platform will be able to adapt with the type of data you select.

* Check your Platform to Benchmark Parameters

Backtesting is done in line with the way a trading strategy is expected to perform with future data. It is accomplished by evaluating the effectiveness of the strategy using historical data. Then, you have to evaluate the effectiveness of the strategy on different variables like the success rate and so on.

The process of backtesting

Once you've considered the issues mentioned above The following step will be to design an effective trading strategy built on the past data. It is possible to build your model with VBA as well as Python and verify it using R. Test your model using the simulator is highly recommended since it can provide insight into problems that occurred in the past. The simulator functions as an actual exchange that can be customized to meet various market conditions.

Backtesting platforms

Beyond visual basic and backtesting, you require backtesting platforms that are specifically tailored to specific strategies. Let's look at various platforms that provide the ability to run speedy backtesting procedures.

TradeStation

In the present day and age it is more than having flashy software to trade markets effectively. You also have access to information and the correct investment method to give you an advantage against other investors. You can do this with the help of TradeStation which is an investment platform which can help you choose to conduct backtesting.

TradeStation is focused on helping traders find the most effective strategy for trading. It makes use of technology and information to help traders make the right decisions. However, it's not going to be a stroll through the woods for beginners and can prove to be extremely difficult to understand.

The minimum amount of investment for this platform is $500 and you must pay a fee of $5 per transaction. You can make investments in penny stocks and mutual funds. You can also invest in stocks, stocks, EFTs, futures, and bonds. The kinds of accounts you can open are IRA tax-free, custodial and trusts.

The platform earns money every time you make a trade. Every trade is $5.00 per equity that you trade. The platform requires you to be an active trader in order to get it to work. As an active trader, you need to complete at least 50 trades each month , or exchange over 5,000 shares per month, or keep an account with a minimum account of $100,000, or you risk being penalized with massive penalties.

The minimum funding requirement for accounts varies based on the class of trade. For EFTs it is required to have an amount of at least $500 to be able to access the platform. Options require a minimum of $2000.

If you sign in to the website (via the internet or the downloadable platform) will show you the most popular videos, the calendar of economic events along with links to workspaces, as well as the company's Twitter feed. It is possible to download the highly customizable desktop software. The web-based platform comes with the majority of the features and is simple to modify to suit your needs.

The data streams in the system are real-time. It is possible to make an order, change or end a trade with keyboard shortcuts. Making changes to the trade is simple and all you have to do is place your mouse over the bid, and then you'll utilize a trade ticket you can edit prior to making the payment.

The Benefits of using TradeStation

Simple Coding Language

Traders who want to gain an advantage over their rivals require a proficiency in the programming language. The great thing is that TradeStation utilizes EasyLanguage which is a basic programming language that is easy to quickly learn. It's a combination between HTML as well as SQL. It is easier to learn if you are already proficient in coding.

Instant Market Updates

TradeStation's RadarScreen offers access to live data sets of 1000 symbols. It gives traders an advantage that is comparable to other traders who use technical trading. The platform is focused on market data that is of high quality to assist you in establishing the best trading strategy. The platform is also stable and will continue to be accessible when markets change.

Technical Analysis

The platform includes over 40 years worth of data to be used for your simulations. This is why it's perfect for testing different strategies by using the data. Additionally, you can use the data to analyze any technical patterns. You can build your automated trading system by using the tools for technical analysis that the platform provides. Additionally, you can earn money with the fully paid loan system for stocks and improve your skills in trading through the many training options available.

It's Fast

The speed at which commands are executed commands makes it an excellent platform for traders wanting to test their strategies. Additionally, it gives access to indicators you can modify based on the strategy you are focusing on.

Discussion Forums

If you're in search of some assistance and answers to your questions they can be asked on the live forum that TradeStation provides. The platform has integrated a forum into the whole system. The discussions that take place within the forum are useful and based on past experience.

Advantages

Requires programming skills

To make the most of the platform in a way that is superior to other traders, it is necessary to be able to master basic programming abilities. While they provide a variety of options out of the box but you must master some programming skills, and you'll see returns.

The absence of an expert analysis

If you thought you would get an expert opinion on the stock, then you'll be disappointed. The platform does not provide any data to assist you in choosing the best stock. Instead it is focused on the use of indicators that assist you in making the best choice. This means that even investors who are serious about their business and who require value-based strategies may not get what they require from the platform.

Costly Courses

The majority of the courses the platform provides are free however, it also provides certain expensive courses that may not be affordable for the majority of beginners.

NinjaTrader

It was established in 2003 and offers software and brokerage services for active traders looking to try out the platform or execute trading operations. It is possible to use the platform at no cost, particularly when you need to do market analysis, charting and trading simulation. But, you must possess a license before placing real trades and using the features that are premium, such as placing advanced types of order as well as backtesting and automated trading. You have the option of leasing and/or purchase software. The features that permit the user to examine the trade's activity with volumes bars, flow and market depth, require you to have an unlimited license.

On the other hand there aren't lots of choices when it comes to purchasing and holding trades as well as investments because the platform doesn't provide a wide range of options regarding research.

This platform is perfect for traders who are active and intend to trade Forex as well as futures. This platform provides you with excellent options for live charts, technical analyses and custom technical indicators.

NinjaTrader provides you with an order execution tool that is chart-based and a variety of applications along with third-party add-ons that you can utilize. While it was initially designed for traders who wish to trade futures, the company has also joined forces with other brokerages to ensure traders can also trade on options Forex as well as stocks and CFDs.

NinjaTrader offers you an interface that is clean and fully customizable charts that are fully customizable. You can change the colors of chart, bar spacing and fonts, as well as the arrangement of the window of the chart. It is easy to include strategies, technical indicators and drawing tools that can be readily added to the chart. Charts also accommodate different bar types like tick or time-based, range or volume bars. Additionally, it offers an array of styles for you to pick from, including OHLC candles, OHLC, Mountain, and Kagi Line.

The platform provides easy to navigate interfaces. One of the best features is Chart Trader, which allows you to plan and manage your charts from within the chart. It can manage all kinds of orders on the platforms like market, limit stop limit, stop limits and stop markets orders as well as one-cancel order.

If you're a lover or automated trading system, the platform provides you semi-automated tools which you can utilize to manage your trades, or automate your trading activities using an Automated Trading Interface entirely.

Real-time data can be obtained for a fee that is based on the type of data feed you need. The data is paid for on a monthly basis. You can play back the data in a tick-by tick basis with the replay feature of the platform. This is great for backtesting trades, trading practice and other types of research.

The platform is simple to download, and it is free to install. The process of installing it is simple and easy, and after you have launched the platform, you are able to add charts, indicators, or charts and modify the colors. It can be a bit tedious for some users, particularly those who are familiar with completely automated systems.

The system is simple to use and gives you access to a variety options of resources and tools. The best part is that the platform offers free webinars to help you get to get started.

One of the greatest advantages of this platform is that it allows you to play with trades. This is possible along with demo accounts, as well as the profit/loss report. This is perfect for backtesting , as well as for those who are new to trading and searching for a place to put into practice what they've learned.

In addition to charts and market depth tools The platform provides the bare minimum of research resources on the basis of its platform. But, because of the platform's focus on active futures trading you have the entire tools needed to trade these markets. You can alter the indicators and the platform, along with other features, are modified to a specific scale. Unfortunately, there aren't any indispensable tools for you and the most notable thing that is missing is financial statements, news and other data that would be ideal for a platform that is professional.

Benefits of NinjaTrader

This platform offers an excellent analysis of technical aspects and charting tools that will provide you with the needed knowledge about the trading.

You'll have access to more than 11,000 apps as well as add-ons to allow you to trade easily and quick.

You can sign up for a demo account to ensure you can try the platform and get a better understanding of what you're getting into.

Advantages

* The platform has the highest fees for signing up, which could be a problem for those who are new to the platform.

The platform offers an easy set-up, and the only drawback is that you need to utilize a different broker to manage other transactions.

* You do not have the ability to access newsfeeds or fundamental information, and research that are not available on the platform.

* It is an encapsulated focus and allows Forex transactions and Futures. You can however utilize the partners of its to exchange stocks as well as other securities.